HR MANAGER'S LEGAL REPORTER
LAWSUIT AVOIDANCE WORKSHOPS

The Seven Secrets of Managers Who Avoid Employee Lawsuits

Stephen D. Bruce, Ph.D.

RANSOM & BENJAMIN PUBLISHERS LLC

Credits

HR Editor:	Maureen M. Gallagher, Editor, HR Managers Legal Reporter
Legal Editor:	Dorit S. Heimer, J.D. Levett, Rockwood & Sanders, P.C. Westport, Connecticut
Copy Editor:	Margaret McCormick
Production Editor:	Jane A. Bruce

This publication is designed to provide accurate and authoritative information in regard to the subject matter covered. It is sold with the understanding that the publisher is not engaged in rendering legal, accounting, or other professional services. If legal advice or other expert assistance is required, the services of a competent professional should be sought. (From a Declaration of Principles jointly adopted by a Committee of the American Bar Association and a Committee of Publishers.)

Copyright

ISBN 0-9645093-2-6

Printed in the United States of America

Questions or comments about this book may be directed to Ransom & Benjamin Publishers, P.O. Box 606, Old Greenwich, CT 06870

1-203-637-0221

Substantial quantity discounts are available from the publisher.

Quick* Table of Contents

*Detailed Table of Contents begins on page ix.

About the Author

Mr. Bruce brings a unique perspective to his writing for managers. As editor-in-chief of a major business publisher, Army officer, college professor, retail manager, and now president of his own company, he understands the ins and outs of management as few can. As editorial manager of such publications as *HR Manager's Legal Reporter, What to Do about Personnel Problems in Your State,* and *BLR's Quick Guide to Employment Law,* Mr. Bruce knows the legal issues that challenge managers, and he conveys the solutions in concise, how-to-do-it style.

His many books for managers include BLR's best-selling *Face to-Face: Every Manager's Guide to Better Interviewing; How to Interview Successfully; BLR's Encyclopedia of Pre-Written Job Descriptions;* and *The Encyclopedia of Performance Appraisal.* Mr. Bruce's articles have appeared in many practical management journals, including *HR Manager's Legal Reporter, HR Horizons, Chemical Engineering, Nursing,* and *Savings Institutions.*

Mr. Bruce holds a B.A. from Davidson College, a Master's from the University of Hartford, and a Ph. D. from the University of Oregon. Former editor-in-chief of Business & Legal Reports, Inc., Mr. Bruce is now the president of Ransom & Benjamin Publishers LLC.

Dedication

This book is dedicated to
my family.

Foreword

Managers beg for lawsuits. They don't realize that they are doing it, but they do.

Managers need training to help themselves avoid employee lawsuits, but the available materials are just too obtuse to do the job. Managers don't want to read through long lists of laws, and who they apply to, and when they were passed, and what every little, tiny detail for compliance is. They just want to know what they should do—and then they'll do it.

What to do

So this is a what-to-do book. And, because of the nature of the laws, a what-not-to-do book.

Action by action

And it is an action book.

What to do when you interview, or when you appraise, or when you are faced with an intolerable situation that seems to cry out for an action, but you're not sure what comes next.

Read, follow, avoid

Read this book, follow the suggestions it contains, and you will avoid lawsuits.

How to Use This Book

This book offers two ways to find information about lawsuit prevention: the Seven Secrets and the Employment Action Quick Reference.

The Seven Secrets

In this section, you'll find the seven basic rules managers and supervisors must follow to manage effectively without causing employee lawsuits.

As you read through this section, you will also build an awareness of the pitfalls that have trapped managers in the past.

The Employment Action Quick Reference

This section is the place to go whenever you are about to engage in an important employee interaction. Material here is organized by action.

Before you interview, appraise, discipline, or fire, look up the topic in this section of *Million Dollar Mouths*, and remind yourself of the do's and don'ts. Go over the checklist before you act.

Detailed Table of Contents

— 1 —
Million Dollar Mouths

Some employers just aren't plagued by employee lawsuits.

Why not? It's simple, really. Their managers actively work to prevent lawsuits, and they avoid doing the things that encourage lawsuits.

We've identified the seven concrete behaviors—we call them the "Seven Secrets"—that make the difference. They're easy to understand. They're easy to follow. They're geared to the work you do every day.

There's no excuse for causing a lawsuit.

MANAGERS BEG FOR LAWSUITS

Surprisingly, when you investigate the underlying causes of most employee lawsuits, *the manager or supervisor begged the employee to sue.* That's right, the manager begged, by

- uttering million dollar words, or
- making million dollar gestures, or
- treating employees unfairly, or

1

- humiliating or harassing or retaliating, or
- violating rules they knew or should have known, or
- crossing a line they shouldn't have crossed, or even
- by doing nothing when he or she should have done something.

'MILLION DOLLAR MOUTHS'

We call managers who cause employee lawsuits "million dollar mouths." Here are some examples of these million dollar managers at work:

Million dollar words

At a New York City bank, an employee of Italian heritage was fired after working three years at the bank. The bank official told him, among other things, that the bank wanted "to have a representative in external business dealings that was a true American." The official also accused the employee of "creating a Mafia shop."

The employee sued the bank on the basis of national origin discrimination.

The jury, upon reflection, apparently didn't like the attitude of the bank manager, as it put the tab for the remarks at $2,600,000.

Million dollar hands

An attorney at a large law firm sexually harassed a new employee by touching her sexually, making inappropriate and lewd remarks, and engaging in such behavior as dropping candies into her blouse pocket.

She complained to management about the behavior, but apparently was not satisfied with their response, as she sued the law firm.

It seems clear that the jury agreed with her, as they fined the law firm $6,900,000.

Importantly, they also sent a message to all managers who believe that they can get away with such behavior—they fined the attorney himself, to the tune of $225,000.

(The jury's award was later reduced to about $3,000,000, but only because that was the amount the woman's attorney had originally asked for.)

$50,000,000 treatment

At one of the country's biggest retailers, a supervisor allowed a demeaning and abusive environment of sexual harassment to continue a little too long.

One of the receiving department employees complained that her supervisor made numerous sexual remarks to her, and permitted other male employees to pinch and kick her. Believing that her complaints were "falling on deaf ears," she sued.

The court didn't think much of her claim for lost wages, awarding $1.

And they didn't think that much more of her claim for humiliation and mental anguish, awarding an additional $35,000.

Then they came to punitive damages, the place in the trial at which they may add an amount to damages that is in their judgment large enough to punish the employer for the actions, and to remind the employer not to do this again.

They thought a lot about punitive damages, finally deciding on a cool $50,000,000 penalty.

ARE YOU BEGGING YOUR EMPLOYEES TO SUE?

You may be a million dollar manager yourself. You may be doing things today that are making your employees think about a lawsuit. Or you may be doing things that will cause them to think about a lawsuit at some future point.

Equally important, you might be *failing* to do the things that you must do to prevent lawsuits.

This book will let you know what you must do—and what you must not do.

IGNORANCE OR ARROGANCE?

If you are about to cause an employee lawsuit, it will probably be because of either ignorance or arrogance.

Ignorance is an unacceptable excuse. Managers must learn how to manage, and avoiding lawsuits is an important part of your basic responsibilities as a manager.

As to arrogance, managers who think they're too big for rules or too important to be disciplined are in for a rude awakening. No organization can ignore employee lawsuits, nor can they afford—from a financial or public image standpoint—to support the managers who cause them.

IT'S EASY TO PREVENT LAWSUITS

Fortunately, it's not hard for you to learn how to prevent employee lawsuits. How can we be so sure?

First, it's not hard to avoid the acts that result in employee lawsuits—once you know what they are.

Second, the acts that cause lawsuits are *not* essential to the successful performance of your job. You can still be an effective manager and avoid lawsuits.

Can I prevent *all* employee lawsuits?

Does this mean that if I follow the rules in this book I can avoid all employee lawsuits?

No, probably not. You can't stop employees from filing suits, even if they have little or no grounds. But you *can* prevent *most* lawsuits by adhering to a few simple rules. And you can significantly reduce the costs of the ones you can't stop.

Can't I WIN the lawsuits?

But surely, you are thinking, employers win a lot of the lawsuits that are filed against them. That's true; you can "win" some of the lawsuits that are filed against you.

That is, you can be declared the victor in court if a case is decided your way. However, it is a surprisingly empty victory. Think about what it's cost in time, productivity, employee morale, community support, and customer image, to say nothing of money. Typically, it costs more than $100,000 just to go to court, often a lot more, even when you "win." And you're not likely to recover any of that.

No, you can't win except by avoiding lawsuits in the first place. This book will show you how.

IT'S YOUR JOB TO PREVENT LAWSUITS

You're the manager! It's *your* responsibility to avoid actions that will result in lawsuits against your organization.

It's *your* responsibility to know what those actions are, and *your* responsibility to supervise and manage without bringing on lawsuits.

This book will give you the guidelines you need.

You must study them.

You must have the self-discipline to adhere to them.

No manager under any circumstances has the right to put his or her organization in million dollar jeopardy.

BE A BETTER MANAGER

I understand, you may be thinking, that it is in my organization's best interest to prevent employee lawsuits, but what about me?

That's the good news—it's in your best interest as well.

The truth is that working to avoid lawsuits will help you to become a better manager.

You can be a better manager AND avoid lawsuits

Frankly, managers and supervisors who follow the rules in this book are more successful in meeting their goals and getting ahead. Those who violate the principles—who treat employees unfairly, play favorites, or engage in harassment or other unlawful actions—are never fully effective. Their people won't support them, and they will spend a lot of time dealing with problems they have brought on themselves, instead of accomplishing their goals.

If you follow the rules in this workshop you will find that your staff's performance and productivity improve, because you are focusing on getting the job done.

You'll gain respect

When you treat employees, colleagues, and customers with respect, you'll find yourself treated with more respect, and you'll get more done.

You'll avoid a lawsuit yourself

Are you thinking, they won't sue me, they'll sue the company?

You're wrong. You could be sued yourself, as an individual. Even if you work for a large corporation, you are not isolated from personal liability for your actions. There are situations in which you could be held personally liable, and your employer might not be able to help you—or might choose not to.

You will avoid a 'career terminating move'

If for no other reason, avoid lawsuits to keep your job. "Career terminating moves" effectively end promising careers like yours. Causing an expensive employee lawsuit that could have been avoided is clearly a career terminating move.

Your organization's policies make clear that the behaviors that result in lawsuits—discrimination, harassment, and retaliation, for example—are unacceptable. If you operate outside those policy boundaries, you'll probably pay for it with your job.

HOW MUCH WILL YOUR SUIT COST?

How much will the lawsuit you cause cost your organization? Fill in the blanks to gauge the impact of an employee lawsuit on your organization.

A. Legal costs of a typical lawsuit (pick a number between 60,000 and 300,000): $ _____

B. Cost of lost productivity (take 10% to 50% of the amount you put down for A above): $ _____

C. Cost of employee morale, community support, customer image problems (10% to 50% of A above.): $ _____

D. Cost of time (take 10 to 30 days of your salary): $ _____

E. Add together A through D. These are the readily identifiable costs of your lawsuit : $ _____

F. Enter the dollar amount of profit from selling one of your typical products, or in one hour of billable time: $ _____

G. Divide E by F: _____

The result is the number of items you must sell or hours you must bill to pay off the cost of an employee lawsuit.

Chart of the Seven Secrets

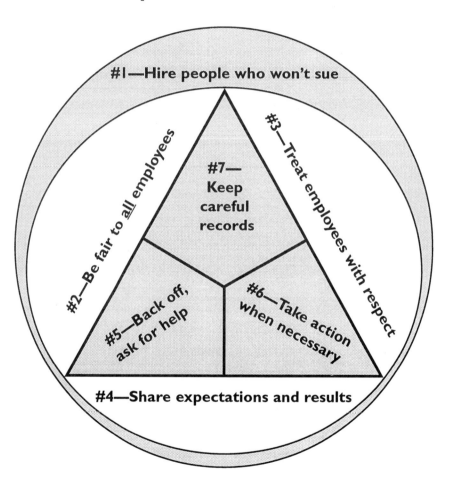

—|||—

The Seven Secrets
of Managers Who
Avoid Employee Lawsuits

There are seven basic behaviors that characterize managers who avoid employee lawsuits. You can easily adopt these behaviors as your own, without giving up your rights as a manager. In fact, you'll probably be a better manager after you start following them.

Are they really secrets?

All available evidence suggests that these behaviors are secrets. The thousands of lawsuits filed in this country every year clearly attest to the fact that most managers don't know them.

When you start learning about the seven secrets, you won't think they sound very "secret." In fact, you'll think they sound like common sense. And they are—which is why it's easy to follow them once you know them.

It doesn't really matter whether you call them secrets or habits or behaviors or what to do; what's important is that you follow them.

—Secret #1—
Hire People Who Won't Sue

This is, of course, the most obvious rule of all. But the simple truth is, if you can avoid hiring employees who will sue you, you've found the simplest and best way to avoid employee lawsuits.

There are two important steps to take to hire people who won't sue:

—First, identify and reject applicants who are prone to bring lawsuits. (There are such people, and you can identify them.)

—Second, devote more attention to making good hiring decisions so you won't have to fire people as often. As firing is often the act that triggers lawsuits, the fewer people you fire, the lower the likelihood of lawsuits.

IDENTIFY AND REJECT

Many—maybe most—problem employees can be identified and weeded out during the hiring process. Avoid two kinds of employees: the kind who like to sue, and the kind who are likely to cause lawsuits, for example, by violence, or by harassment.

More often than not, says one attorney, when I go back into the work history of an employee who has sued, or who has caused a lawsuit, I find clear evidence of prior problems:

- Employees who sue often have sued before;

- Employees who commit violence often have committed violent acts in the past; and

- Employees who harass or who make trouble often have harassed or made trouble for other employers.

Evidence is often in plain sight

Often evidence indicating a troublemaker is right on the application or the resume. There may be gaps in the employment history, or a number of jobs that lasted only a few months, or "red flag" reasons for leaving prior jobs such as "poor management," or "disagreed with policies," or "organization poorly run." Perhaps there are good explanations, but at the least these are important warning signs to be followed up with thorough questioning during your selection process.

Evidence is readily available

In other cases, information that would cause you to reject an applicant is readily available from outside sources — phone calls to former supervisors and routine background checks — but only if you call the former supervisors or request that the background checks be accomplished.

You can avoid hiring suit-happy employees

The bottom line is that a little effort up front in the hiring process will help you avoid hiring people who will bring, or cause, lawsuits. Here are some tips:

- Ask what, why, who, where, when questions. Follow through for details.

- Check for problem indicators on any of the documents. Look for gaps in the employment history, too many jobs in too short a period.

- Do consistent, detailed reference checks. Be sure to talk to direct supervisors. Ask about performance on the job and avoid asking any illegal questions (see discussion of appropriate questions under "Be Fair").

- Engage a professional agency to conduct background checks appropriate to the position.

- Compare all the information you have. Are resume' and application consistent with each other and with information gained during background checks, reference checks, and interviews?

Avoid the ducks

One expert says, if it looks like a duck and walks like a duck, it's a duck. Don't hire ducks. That is, if you feel there might be problems, there probably are. Trust your gut instincts. If you feel in your gut that something is not right, you could be reacting to a problem that you have identified but haven't yet been able to articulate. Trust your gut. Don't hire. Why take a chance?

MAKE BETTER HIRING DECISIONS

Putting more attention on your hiring decisions will result in better hires—employees more likely to be able to do their jobs successfully. That means you'll fire fewer employees, which in turn means fewer lawsuits.

Know what you are looking for

The key to better hires is knowing precisely

- what functions are required to do the job,

- what characteristics, skills and
  experience are necessary to do the job, and

- how you'll determine whether applicants
  meet the requirements.

Surprisingly, many managers start interviewing with no clear idea of what they are looking for!

But if you don't know what you are looking for, you'll have no basis for evaluating candidates. That makes for weak hires, and in fact, can strengthen a lawsuit. If someone claims discrimination because you didn't hire him or her, it will be difficult to rationally explain your choices, and to refute the discrimination claim.

The bottom line: hire the right person the first time and you won't have to fire.

'We'll see if it works out'

"Well, let's hire someone and we'll see how it works out. If they can't do the job, we can fire them."

"We'll hire three and keep the best one."

These are the voices of lazy managers who aren't taking the trouble to do the job right. They are begging for lawsuits. Furthermore, they are going to waste a tremendous amount of the organization's resources whether there's a lawsuit or not.

Be fair in recruiting

There are a number of guidelines governing the employment process that you must follow to avoid lawsuits. See the section entitled "Be Fair to All Applicants and Employees" for detailed information.

CAN YOU AVOID *ALL* TROUBLEMAKERS?

Probably not all troublemakers, but it's worth the effort even if you avoid only one. Actually, it's worth the effort even if you don't avoid any, because, at the very least, you'll establish your good faith effort to avoid problems.

For example, should an employee turn violent, you'll be able to demonstrate that you did what you could to screen candidates and avoid hiring people with violent tendencies.

Conversely, you do not want to be on the witness stand explaining how you never quite got around to doing reference checks on one of your employees who just committed a violent act, an act that he or she had committed before at a former place of employment.

YOU NEVER KNOW

One attorney tells the story of a client who was being sued by an employee the client had just fired. Although the termination was for poor performance, the former employee claimed that he was fired because he had reported regulatory violations to the authorities.

In preparing for the case, the attorney contacted five former employers. All five had been victims of the same scam.

Obviously, not one of these employers had bothered to pursue reference checks on this employee.

HOW IS YOUR HIRING RECORD?

Check if:

☐ any of your employees have sued your organization.

☐ any of your hires have left the organization soon after joining.

☐ you had to terminate or encourage the resignation of any of your recent hires.

If you checked any of the boxes above, think through the hiring process you used.

What should you have discovered before hiring that you didn't?

What sign did you ignore that you should have paid attention to?

What could you have done to have spotted the trouble before you hired?

Did you:

☐ know what you were looking for?

☐ ensure to the best of your ability that the candidate was qualified and could do the job?

Reference and background checks
In your background checking, do you:
☐ contact former employers?
☐ speak personally with former supervisors?
☐ check out any gaps on the resume?
☐ verify degrees, certificates, etc.?
☐ do motor vehicle checks?
☐ conduct criminal record checks?

Do you have:

☐ positions in which individual employees visit clients in their homes?
☐ safety-sensitive positions such as bus drivers?
☐ positions in which adults work with children?

If so, what special care do you take with your records and background checks?

—Secret #2—
Be Fair to <u>All</u> Employees

Fairness—not legality—is the most basic issue in avoiding lawsuits. Why? Because fairness is what matters to juries.

THINK THE WAY A JURY THINKS

Many of the most costly cases in employment law are decided by juries. Although judges carefully instruct jury members in the finer points of law involved in their cases, the truth is that juries are generally swayed more by a desire for fairness than by a desire for technical legal correctness. Juries ask this question:

Was this act by the employer fair to the employee?

And if it was not , the jury asks:

What can we do to remedy the situation?

And sometimes, they get to ask a third question:

How can we punish the employer so this won't happen again?

For instance, let's say your company promises a long-time employee something, then doesn't deliver. The employee suffers a loss and eventually sues. You argue that there was no legal contract, so you had no legal oblig-ation. The employee says simply that he or she trusted your company and that its actions weren't fair.

You may be technically right, but with whom do you think the jury will side? The big, bad, deep-pockets employer who treated a long-term employee shabbily? Or the poor, long-suffering, hard-working employee?

Who is the typical jury member?

Who will you be facing in the jury box? Not 12 corpo-rate managers who think as you do. More likely, lower level workers or retired workers—or, worse, laid off work-ers—who are much more likely to sympathize with your employee than with you.

What does a jury think fairness means?

To avoid actions that generate lawsuits, think like a jury member—think fairness as you deal with your employees. When the jury asks, was the employer fair, you want their answer to be, yes, it was.

Read through these questions a jury member might be asking about an action you might be taking today.

- Did the employee know what the employer expected of her?

- Did she know what consequences could result from her actions?

- Did the employer make her a promise?

- Did the employee get what was promised to her?

- Did a manager take action before finding out the facts ?

- Was the action taken the same action as was taken in similar circumstances in the past?
- Were the decision criteria fair?
- Did you follow policies and rules?
- Was the action taken against the employee a surprise?
- Did the employee have a chance to explain?
- Did the manager or organization trick or deceive the employee in any way?
- Was any important information withheld?
- Was there a reasonable expectation that was not met?
- Did you "kick the employee while he was down"?
- Did you "add insult to her injury"?
- Did you retaliate against an employee for doing something any employee should have the right to do?

THINK CONSISTENCY, REASONABLENESS, EQUALITY

There are three legs upon which fair treatment of employees rests: consistency, reasonableness, and equality. Here's what you need to know about each.

Be consistent

Consistency means that for any given set of facts or circumstances, your actions toward similar employees are the same.

For example, if you suspend one employee for missing the third day in a row without calling in, but then don't suspend the next employee who fails to call by the third day, you're setting up an unfair situation. If that employee turns around and complains that you did this because he or she is a member of a protected group, will you be able to support your decision? It won't be easy if you haven't been consistent.

One attorney suggests the following test of your consistency: you'll be able to tell how consistent you really are when one of your "stars" falls. For example, does your top salesperson get the same discipline as the least successful salesperson?

Be reasonable

Reasonableness means that a reasonable, neutral observer would find your action within the bounds of normal behavior.

For example, for a minor infraction, did you discharge a long-time, loyal employee? "That doesn't seem fair" is what the jury will think, even if you and your lawyer are thinking "this is an employment-at-will firm and we can fire whomever we want whenever we want."

Be equal

Equal treatment is the most important part of being fair. It's at the root of many employee lawsuits.

Lawsuits alleging any form of discrimination are based on failure to treat employees equally. This includes overt discrimination, of course, but also other more subtle forms of discrimination, such as stereotyping, patronizing, and favoritism.

The basic rule: give all your employees equal treatment.

More specifically, give all your employees equal treatment regardless of their belonging to any group or category below.

Race or National Origin

Discrimination based on race or national origin is, of course, illegal and should be unacceptable to all organizations. And it is certainly unacceptable to juries.

Race and national origin discrimination includes employment actions such as hiring and promoting, and also harassment on the basis of national origin.

Race generally indicates belonging to one of the standard racial groupings defined as:

• White (not of Hispanic origin)

• Black (not of Hispanic origin)

• Hispanic

• Asian or Pacific Islanders

• American Indian or Alaskan Natives

National origin generally means the country of one's origin or one's ancestors' origin.

Creed or Religion

Discrimination based on religion is a growing problem for employers. If your employees request religious accommodations, or if they are practicing their religions at work in ways that offend other employees or interfere with work, seek guidance from your HR department on your organization's policies. Note also that courts are beginning to recognize the concept of harassment in the context of religion.

Sex

Sex discrimination can be manifested in terms of preferences or biases. There are very few cases in which you may legally exercise preference based on sex in employment decisions. For example, you may not hire only women or only men or favor one sex in connection with job promotions or other benefits.

Sex discrimination also includes its special form, sex harassment. There is a detailed discussion of sexual harassment below in the section, "Treat Employees with Respect."

Age

Age discrimination laws generally protect people over age 40 from adverse employment actions based on their age. This includes, in most cases, protection from termination at a certain age.

Be especially aware of appearances. Avoid any lighthearted comments like "time to move over and let the younger people have their day" or "I'm giving the promotion to someone who is going to be around a while longer."

Marital Status

In general, avoid making employment decisions based upon an applicant's or employee's marital status. Although marital status as such is not protected by federal law, it is protected by many state laws, and discrimination can verge upon sex discrimination as well.

Sexual Orientation

While actually protected by law in only a few states and localities, more and more employers are forbidding discrimination on the basis of sexual orientation as a matter of policy. It's an issue of attracting the best employees and of corporate image and employee morale.

Disability

If you base any employment decisions or actions (recruiting, appraising, training, promotion, termination, etc.)—in whole or in part—on whether or not someone has a disability, you are begging for a lawsuit. Some of the obvious disabilities may include:

- Illegal drug use
- Alcohol abuse
- AIDS
- Mental incapacities
- Stress
- Back pain
- Weight

Understanding what is and is not a disability is one of the toughest problems managers face. And the requirements for "reasonable accommodation" of disabilities are just about as tough.

The law provides protection in certain circumstances and not in others—check with your HR department when you encounter disabilities. And pay careful attention to the section below on interviewing applicants with disabilities.

Pregnancy

In general, treat pregnant women the same way you treat any other employee with a disability. This means that you may not refuse to hire, refuse to promote, or fire a woman because she is pregnant. You may not force a pregnant woman to go on leave as long as she can work. When one of your employees announces her pregnancy, contact the HR department so you can be sure of the policies that apply.

Various State-Law-Based Prohibitions

Most states have their own laws prohibiting various types of discrimination. For example, sexual orientation, child-bearing capacity, public assistance status, off-duty smoking, and filing of a workers' compensation claim may be protected behaviors or categories in your state. (See the appendix on state law for more information.)

Equal treatment doesn't mean 'kid gloves'

"Don't discriminate" doesn't mean "don't manage." You can—and must—take action against those who don't perform or who break the rules. You just can't take action *because* of one of the characteristics listed above.

Equal treatment doesn't mean the same treatment

Does "equal treatment" mean that all employees have to get the same raise, the same evaluation? No. The point is to apply the same rules, policies, and procedures to each employee, and to ensure that each employee has the same opportunity for consideration as every other employee.

HOW MANAGERS DISCRIMINATE

Discrimination comes in many forms, some obvious and overt, some subtle and hard to spot. A manager or supervisor who engages in any form of discrimination in the workplace is begging for a lawsuit. Here's what to avoid:

Overt discrimination (I don't like **X's**)

This is the out-in-the-open type of discrimination that most people think of when they hear the word. For example:

I don't like to work with [women, men, old people, white people, black people, Asian people, disabled people].

My customers don't like to deal with [women, men, old people, white people, black people, Asian people, disabled people].

I don't think [women, men, old people, white people, black people, Asian people, disabled people] can do this type of job.

I don't hire [women, men, old people, white people, black people, Asian people, disabled people].

I don't like to hire [young women because they get pregnant and go on leave].

I'm not promoting [anyone over 40—they don't have enough energy].

Stereotypes (**X's** can't **X**)

Stereotyping usually takes the form of "X's can't X."
Women aren't strong enough. Men aren't compassionate enough. X's aren't smart enough.

Evaluate individuals' abilities, skills, and experience against requirements.

Patronize/paternalize/maternalize (**X's** shouldn't **X**)

This is a special form of stereotyping that seems well-intentioned, but is, in general, discriminatory. For example,

Terry is active in the community; he/she won't want to relocate.

29

Parents with young children shouldn't travel.

Women shouldn't travel alone.

*Pregnant women can't travel, lift, move,
be subjected to pressure.*

'Avoidance' Discrimination

Some managers try to play a game of avoidance discrimination. They say, if I can get in trouble talking to X's, no problem. I'll never talk to them. Never take them along, never communicate with them at all.

Don't use this thinking; it is discriminatory and it won't fly.

Play favorites (I always hire my friends)

You've got groups with whom you feel comfortable—people you get together with for sports, perhaps. You get along with them, and you always turn to that group when you need to hire.

And you've got friends at work with whom you're comfortable. They always get the plum projects, the ones that put them in line for bonuses and promotions. And they get the social invitations.

De facto (Gee, I just never seem to hire X's)

One of the more subtle forms of discrimination is called "de facto." In these situations, there are never any direct statements against hiring or promoting certain types of people—it just never seems to happen. For example, you're not against hiring women in a certain job, but, although many qualified women have applied, of the last 50 hires, all 50 were men.

Unequal opportunity

Part of fairness is equal opportunity. In all employment actions, be sure that all eligible employees have an equal chance to apply. Make sure they know how to apply. Make sure they know what it takes to advance, how to acquire it, and how to demonstrate it.

Include everyone in business social events, get-togethers, or informal sessions where these situations are discussed.

Reverse Discrimination

Reverse discrimination means discriminating against someone as a result of your attempts not to discriminate against someone else. You probably don't have significant exposure unless you have a very strong, quota-type program favoring one protected group.

THE EASY WAY TO BE FAIR— FOCUS ON THE JOB

There are a lot of ways to discriminate. Fortunately, there's an easy way to ensure that you're being fair to all employees. When you're interacting with employees or making business decisions that affect them, *focus on the job*.

For example, focus on an applicant's qualifications for an opening or an employee's qualifications for a promotion or assignment to a project team, or on the success the employee has had in meeting goals, in enhancing productivity, in landing new business.

When taking actions that affect employees, set out in front of you your mission, your goals and objectives, and the business requirements you need to meet.

31

Set out the nature of the job or task to be done and the skills and abilities and knowledge needed to accomplish it.

Then set out available applicants or employees and evaluate their experience, qualifications, skills, and abilities against your goals and objectives.

Make your decision based on that information.

Employment decisions include the whole gamut of employee actions. The following provides tips to use when taking any of these actions.

Note that the role of the HR or personnel department varies from organization to organization. In some, the HR department may take control of many of the activities described below, while in others every manager has independent responsibility. Be sure you know how the relationship works in your organization before starting out.

BE FAIR IN YOUR RECRUITING

Recruiting consists of a series of activities, including setting job standards, advertising, interviewing, selecting, offering, negotiating, and orienting. Improper actions during any of these steps can sow the seeds for a future lawsuit.

Setting requirements

The first step in recruiting is to set forth the requirements for the open position. The legal jeopardy here is inadvertent discrimination. You may, if you set requirements that aren't really necessary (such as a college degree for a clerical position), exclude a disproportionate number of members of a particular protected group. So focus on meaningful requirements of the position's essential functions. Avoid any mention of age, sex, race, religion, disability or national origin, or any characteristic protected by your state law (for example, marital status, or public assistance status).

If you want to set standards such as area of residence, specific diplomas, language facility, or physical requirements, check with the HR department.

Seeking candidates

In seeking candidates for your opening, determine the scope of your campaign (that is, local, regional, national) and then advertise broadly. You would like it to be clear that you made efforts to attract a wide variety of candidates.

Again, avoid any mention of age, race, religion, sex, or other protected characteristic. In addition, beware of terms such as waitress or busboy that seem to demand applicants only of one sex.

Follow any policies your organization has concerning internal recruiting.

If your organization has an affirmative action program, familiarize yourself with its contents and follow its guidelines throughout the recruiting process. Include "Equal Opportunity Employer" in your ads.

Evaluating applicants

In evaluating resumés and selecting which applicants to interview, stay job-focused—what are the requirements of the job, and how well can this candidate fulfill them?

Could you justify on the basis of your job requirements the choices you made?

Interviewing

Interestingly, one of the biggest sources of interview failure is not having clarified for yourself what the job entails. This can lead to unhelpful general discussions on non-job topics like sports, or dangerous non-job topics, like family plans or church. It's easy to fall into these discussions if you haven't planned your interview.

Be sure that you know what you are looking for, and develop a series of questions that will let you determine whether applicants can meet your requirements. Plan to ask these questions of each candidate.

In addition, prepare questions for each individual candidate that will help you explore particulars of that candidate's background as revealed in the resume', or phone screening, or on the application.

Stick to questions about the job, experience for the job, and other work-focused questions. Try to avoid discussions about non-job topics. It's information you really don't want. Any information you gather about family planning, religious beliefs, or racial background could be ammunition for a future lawsuit. Information about disabilities also is potentially dangerous. See the following section for further discussion of this issue.

What can you interview about?

It may seem that there's nothing you can ask about, but that is not true. You can get the information you need to make a decision; however, at the same time, you must be careful about what you ask. In general, you will be all right if you stick to a discussion of job requirements. Here are some guidelines:

Personal characteristics

Age. Ask only whether the person is of a legal age to work.

Height and weight. Ask only if the characteristics are job related, which is rare.

Race or color. Do not ask.

Photos. Do not ask for a photo of any applicant.

Disabilities

Dealing with disabled persons in the interview is a very delicate task. The Americans with Disabilities Act (ADA) has spelled out rather strict guidelines, which you should follow carefully.

Note: these guidelines are somewhat obtuse and confusing. Nevertheless, you need to familiarize yourself with them—there is a lot of litigation potential from failure to adhere to these rules. If you are confused, seek out the advice of your HR manager before you interview.

You may ask whether a candidate can perform the essential functions of the position *with or without* accommodation. However, you may *not* ask whether the candidate has a disability or what the disability is.

As a result of guidance issued in November 1995,

IF

> you reasonably believe a person has a need for accommodation because of an obvious disability (for example, is in a wheel chair, or has an obvious vision problem),

OR

you reasonably believe that accommodation would be required by a disability an applicant has disclosed to you,

OR

if the candidate asks for accommodation,

THEN you may ask

whether the person needs reasonable accommodation,

AND

what type of reasonable accommodation is needed to perform the job.

If the applicant says he or she will need accommodation, you may then ask questions about the type of accommodation needed. For example, for a person with a vision disability who requests software to make screen images bigger, you could inquire about the availability of the software and its compatibility with your system software. You still may not directly inquire about the nature of the disability.

As another example, if an applicant reveals to you that he or she needs an accommodation of periodic breaks to take medication, you may ask about the length and frequency of the breaks, but not about the underlying disease that requires the medication.

If the applicant, when asked whether an accommodation is needed, responds no, you may not ask further about accommodation. You may ask the applicant to demonstrate or tell how he or she would perform the tasks of the position, *if* you ask all applicants to perform the same demonstration.

Sickness and Attendance

You may not inquire how many days a person missed due to illness, because this may tend to elicit information about a disability. However, since there may be many reasons for not meeting attendance requirements, you may ask, after providing an applicant with your attendance requirements, whether he or she can meet the requirements. In addition, you may ask about the applicant's attendance record, that is, you may ask, "How many days were you absent?" You also may ask questions designed to detect whether an applicant abused leave. For example, you may ask, "How many Mondays or Fridays were you absent last year for any reason except approved vacation leave?"

Again, dealing with disabilities in the interview is a difficult challenge; talk to your HR department if you have any concerns about what you should and should not do.

Availability

Ask if applicants can work the normal hours of the job, whether they are available for overtime (if overtime is a requirement of the position), and whether they have obligations that would prevent them from business travel.

Avoid questions such as, "Are you available for work on Saturdays or Sundays?" (could be religious discrimination) or "Do you have children or child-care responsibilities?" (could be discriminatory, especially if asked just of women).

Background

Birthplace and citizenship. Ask only whether the applicant is legally authorized to work in the U.S.

Residence. Generally, do not inquire about where people live or what type of housing they occupy.

Marital status. Avoid asking applicants their marital status or whether they are married.

Name/name change. Ask if there is additional information that you need about the applicant's name to verify education and experience.

Personal finances. Do not ask about finances, including questions about home ownership or financial problems such as garnishment or bankruptcy.

Relatives. If you have a policy concerning nepotism or hiring of relatives, you may recite the policy and ask if the policy would apply to the applicant.

Religion. Do not ask any questions about religion.

Education and experience

Education. Ask about highest grade completed, academic, vocational, or professional school attended, and certificates and diplomas earned, if required for the job.

Language. If the position requires language fluency, you may ask about written and spoken language ability. Do not ask, "Which language is your native tongue?" or any similar question.

Military service. You may ask about the applicant's status as a U.S. veteran, and whether any military experience helped prepare the candidate for the position sought.

Organizations, clubs, associations. Ask if applicants have any more information they would like to present to further demonstrate their ability to do the job in question. Try not to ask about memberships that would indicate the applicant's race, religion, or disability, or identify any other protected characteristic.

Arrest and conviction records. Generally, ask only about convictions. As far as barring employment based on a conviction, several states have laws that prohibit discrimination on the basis of arrests and convictions unless they are related to the job. Many employers include a statement on their application forms to the effect that a conviction will not necessarily be a bar to employment.

References

Asking for references is all right. Do not, however, specifically ask for a clergy reference. Normally there will be a statement on the application which authorizes you to verify all information and contact references, and authorizes them to release information to you.

Record interview reactions immediately

Although it is permissible to take notes during the interview, many interviewers prefer to jot notes down after the interviewee leaves. In either case, do not delay making notes. If you wait until you have conducted several interviews, you'll forget who was who and who said what.

Application form may be a guide

Your organization's application form, if it is updated regularly to conform to changing laws, may serve as a good guide for areas of inquiry.

Testing applicants

Employers use a variety of tests to evaluate applicants' suitability for positions. These tests include everything from skill tests such as a keyboarding test, to personality and honesty tests, to lie detector, or polygraph, tests.

As testing is an area where varying and technical state requirements govern the legality of the testing, check with your HR department before administering tests to applicants. When you do administer tests, be sure that they are administered equally to all applicants for the same position.

HR DEPARTMENT ACTIONS

There are a number of other legal issues surrounding the hiring process that normally fall under the personnel or HR department. For example, they must ensure that new employees comply with the requirements of immigration laws. If organizations are affected by legal affirmative action requirements or policies related to equal opportunity, they must follow certain rules in soliciting candidates, maintaining certain records concerning applicants, and following other selection procedures.

In general, you will not be responsible for these functions, but you should certainly cooperate with the HR department in administering them and providing information.

PERFORMANCE APPRAISAL AND EVALUATION

Be sure that you fully understand your evaluation system and that you have clearly communicated it to your employees.

Set goals for each employee for the period being reviewed. Without goals and standards, it's hard to say much about performance, and what you say won't carry very far in court. If there was nothing to measure performance against, how did you decide?

• Ensure that goals are specific and measurable.

- Ensure that the measurement criteria and the link to the reward system are clear.

- Let your performance appraisal flow from an evaluation of performance against goals.

- Discuss successes and shortcomings from the job perspective—not a personality perspective For example, say, you're 35 minutes late, rather than you're lazy; or you missed the deadline, rather than you don't care).

- Avoid any comment that could suggest a discriminatory attitude, for example:

   —You women are all alike,

   —You men are all alike,

   —You X's have always been good at ...

   —Y's always seem to have trouble with that.

EMPLOYEE TRAINING

If there is something that an employee must do to be considered for training programs, be sure all employees know what it is and how to do it.

In selecting employees for training programs or other development opportunities, be sure that all eligible employees are considered.

The selection system must be fair, both in actuality and appearances. It isn't enough to say that you are fair. If you reject every member of a protected class, time after time, you are in trouble, no matter how careful you are in your selection procedures and no matter how loudly you protest your fairness.

COMPENSATION AND PAY

Your organization probably has guidelines for compensation management. From your standpoint, the lawsuit prevention side of compensation is primarily an issue of consistency and fairness.

Be sure to observe pay and overtime rules under the Fair Labor Standards Act (FLSA). Some aspects of the FLSA are technical, such as rules for waiting time, travel time, report-in pay, and so on. Whenever employees are working for you or doing anything for your benefit and you are not paying them or are not paying the full rate, check with the HR department to be sure you are acting legally.

Be sure you evaluate employees' performance and rewards according to on-the-job accomplishments and performance against goals and not because of favoritism or discrimination.

In particular, be sure that men and women—or members of any group—are paid the same rates for the same work. Similarly, check your payroll records and pay rates to be sure that no group is singled out for extra low or extra high pay.

EMPLOYEE DEVELOPMENT OPPORTUNITIES

Selection for development opportunities also offers situations in which unfair actions may lead to legal trouble.

These development opportunities include any kinds of special assignments, which may be mundane or exciting, but which have the potential to affect careers.

For example,

- Who will accompany the president on a
  trip to woo a new client?

- Who will serve on a reengineering committee?
- Who will help to select the new computer system?
- Who will serve on the special task force?
- Who will open the new facility?

Any number of such assignments come up at every organization, and all such assignments have the potential to help people move ahead.

Exercise care in parceling out these plum assignments. Don't let a discriminatory pattern develop.

On the other side, at most organizations, there are tasks that no one wants, tasks that are viewed as dead ends, or just drudgery.

Fairness dictates that these assignments should be shared equally as well.

PROMOTIONS AND NEW ASSIGNMENTS

Let employees know what is required to move ahead, and how to apply or be considered for opportunities.

When selecting employees to promote or to move on to other assignments, put all eligible employees in the selection pool, and consider all eligible employees fairly against the criteria you have established.

DISCIPLINE

Again, strive for consistency, reasonableness, and fairness in your discipline system. Careful documentation is vitally important in these proceedings.

- Be sure that you know the rules yourself. Every time you act without knowing company policy, you run the risk of violating it. That leads to inconsistent treatment of employees, and inconsistency makes it hard to fight lawsuits.

- Especially before taking serious disciplinary action, seek advice or approval from your HR department.

- Determine whether the employee might have a claim of discrimination, or whether you might appear to be discriminating.

- Determine whether the employee has recently filed any type of complaint against the organization, or exercised some other right. Could your discipline be viewed as retaliation?

- Conduct your disciplinary actions in private.

- Maintain dignity and respect. Do not shout, cow, or brutally attack an employee, especially in front of others.

TERMINATIONS TAKE SPECIAL CARE

Terminations are probably the most unpleasant part of management's role. However, since terminations are the trigger for many lawsuits, it is best to take your time in evaluating the appropriateness of a termination, and planning and carrying it out.

Generally, you will want to check with the HR department for guidance before you terminate an employee. Federal and state laws, as well as seniority and other practices, may need to be observed, and there will be other important issues to consider if you want to minimize the chance of an employee lawsuit.

In evaluating and planning a termination, take the following steps at a minimum.

Analyze the individual's record

Review the person's record. Does material in the record support your decision?

Would a lesser punishment (a suspension, for example) be more appropriate?

Has he or she filed any complaints recently, such that you might be considered guilty of retaliating?

Is he or she a member of a protected class who might appear to be being discriminated against?

Is he or she likely to sue?

Analyze the broad perspective

In addition to analyzing the individual's record, take a look at the termination in the context of the whole organization.

Have others who committed the same offense been terminated?

In general, would this action be considered fair?

Create a severance package

Severance packages may be effective lawsuit preventers, especially when you think an employee is very angry and may be in a frame of mind to sue.

What sort of severance will you offer? Your organization probably has standard policies, but there may be cases in which a substantial severance package, coupled with a well-drafted release form, may be the prudent thing to do. Think of it as a form of insurance.

Agree on references

If the employee is to be allowed to resign, which is not unusual, clarify what references, if any, the organization will give.

Plan the termination

Pull all information together, plan what you are going to say, and schedule the termination meeting in a private place. Think through what the person will do after the meeting. (Go back to his or her office? Go home? Go to HR? Go to a counselor?)

Consider a witness

If you suspect that your action may cause problems, either in the form of a violent reaction or of a lawsuit, consider the advisability of asking another manager or member of the HR department to join you for the termination.

Act with dignity

A termination is not likely to be a pleasant experience for anyone involved, but at the least, you can treat the person being terminated with dignity and respect. Do not be vicious or derogatory or uncaring. There's nothing to be gained and a lot to lose.

Conduct an exit interview

As mentioned elsewhere in this workshop, the opportunity to "vent" can be helpful, and early warning about an employee likely to sue can allow for intervention by your organization before an opposing attorney gets hold of the case.

REMEMBER: APPEARANCES COUNT

Again, the reminder: in employee lawsuits, appearances often count as strongly as fact. Therefore, in addition to avoiding actions actually based on forbidden factors, you must avoid actions that *appear* to be based on these factors.

For example: Your system for selecting employees for advanced training seems on its face to be fair and objective, yet, although your candidates for training are half X's and half Y's, you always select Y's for this position. You believe that each individual decision was justified, but the appearance is otherwise, and it could get you into trouble.

YOUR DEPARTMENT'S TALLY

Fill in the tally sheet below showing your division or department's supervisory and line worker employees by race and by sex.

Are there any conclusions a jury might draw that you wouldn't want them to?

Cautions:

1. Depending on the outcome of your tally, you may have created a document that should not be kept on file. It could end up as a piece of evidence.

2. Different locales have different racial make-ups. What might be considered a "good" tally in one area may not be a good tally in another. Confer with your HR manager about your results if you are not sure of their implications.

Tally #1

		Supervisory	Line Worker
Race	American Indian or Alaskan Natives	_____	_____
	Asian or Pacific Islanders	_____	_____
	Black (not of Hispanic origin)	_____	_____
	Hispanic	_____	_____
	White (not of Hispanic origin)	_____	_____
Sex	Male	_____	_____
	Female	_____	_____

Tally #2

Pick a selection activity you recently performed (hiring, selecting for training, promotion, etc.)

On the second chart, write in the totals for the people you considered and the people you selected (example: you interviewed 19 people, and selected three).

Note: The cautions on the previous page apply to this tally as well.

		Supervisory	Line Worker
Race	American Indian or Alaskan Natives	_____	_____
	Asian or Pacific Islanders	_____	_____
	Black (not of Hispanic origin)	_____	_____
	Hispanic	_____	_____
	White (not of Hispanic origin)	_____	_____
Sex	Male	_____	_____
	Female	_____	_____

Do your selection groups and your final selections seem appropriate in light of the makeup of your organization?

Presumably, you're comfortable with your reasons for each individual decision. But what will a jury think of your actions as a whole?

—Secret #3—
Treat Employees with Respect

A lot of power comes along with being a manager. You can push your employees surprisingly far; employees who want to keep their jobs and feed their families will take a lot of abuse. However, every employee has a breaking point, and an employee who feels oppressed, mistreated, or abused is more likely to sue than other employees.

In fact, the triggering event for many lawsuits is an act of disrespect. An employee who wouldn't have thought about suing is humiliated or harassed or embarrassed, or just frustrated that no one will listen, and decides "I'm not taking this anymore; I deserve a little respect." Suddenly, you're facing an expensive lawsuit—and often a jury that feels great empathy for your employee.

These lawsuits are easily avoided, however, because there's nothing difficult about being respectful of your employees. It won't interfere with getting your goals accomplished; in fact, it probably will improve your group's performance.

Respect covers a lot of ground. The fundamental first level is respecting employees' legal rights. The second level has to do with respect for person and privacy, or just plain treating employees decently. Finally, there's knowing when to keep your mouth closed and when to keep your ears open.

RESPECT EMPLOYEES' RIGHTS

All employees have certain legal rights which you must observe. Some rights are directly given by law, while others may be assumed by those judging your actions on the basis of fairness. For most organizations, both federal and state laws apply, and the most restrictive law usually takes precedence.

Note: This listing covers the basic rights of your employees; individual laws and court decisions which provide these rights generally have specific provisions and limitations. Your safest bet is to follow these guidelines unless you are sure you are in the right. If you are not sure whether or not you are stepping on an employee's rights, check with your HR department before you respond or take action.

Rights given by law

Among the rights that employees enjoy by law are the following:

Civic duties

- the right to vote.

- the right to perform jury duty.

- in some states, the right to answer a subpoena to testify in court.

Safe workplace

- the right to a safe workplace environment (under the Occupational Safety and Health Act or similar state acts).

- the right to report unsafe situations in the workplace without retaliation.

Illegal actions

- the right not to perform an illegal act. For example, a worker who refuses to falsify testimony or participate in a price-fixing scheme may be protected from termination.

- the right to report illegal activity (engage in whistle-blowing) without retaliation.

Uphold the public interest

- in some states, the right to act in the public interest. Workers who are doing the "right thing," even though there may be no specific law protecting their action, may be protected.

Legal actions

- in some states, the right to engage in legal activities outside of work. Although many of these laws were passed to prohibit employers from discriminating against smokers, they may also protect other social activities.

Garnishment

- the right not to be disciplined as a result of having had one's pay garnished, that is, reduced by an amount that the employer is ordered to pay to someone else as a result of a court order.

Reputation
- the right not to be defamed (to have false statements about a worker "published").

Medical leave
- the right to unpaid leave in certain circumstances (for example, under the Family and Medical Leave Act).

Disability accommodation
- the right to have disabilities accommodated within reason (under the Americans with Disabilities Act).

Workers' Compensation
- the right to file workers' compensation claims after an accident or injury without retaliation.

Freedom from discrimination
- the right to treatment free from illegal discrimination (see detailed discussion of discrimination above under "Be Fair").

Freedom from harassment
- the right to treatment free from illegal harassment (see detailed discussion of sexual harassment below under "Respect Employees' Persons").

Union activity
- the right to participate in certain union activities (under the National Labor Relations Act).

Special rules apply to unionized organizations. Any manager or supervisor operating in a union-organized facility or who deals with organized employees must be trained in the rules that govern the management/worker relationship, and must be thoroughly familiar with the union contract and how its provisions are interpreted.

For example, in a discipline meeting, the accused employee may have the right to union representation during the meeting. There may be restrictions on how you can assign work or what you yourself may do.

Even in non-unionized organizations, there are certain rights that employees have in organizing. If you hear or suspect that employees are engaging in union-organizing activity or if union organizers are around, contact the HR department. There are counter-union actions you may take, but they are carefully prescribed by law. Find out the limitations before you act.

Political activity

- in some states, the right to engage in certain political activity.

Compensation

- the right to pay and overtime according to certain rules (under the Fair Labor Standards Act). As mentioned above, there are some technical aspects to the FLSA. Whenever employees are working for you or doing anything for your benefit and you are not paying them or are not paying the full rate (for example, if employees are running errands, or on call, or volunteering to put in extra hours), check with the HR department to be sure you are fulfilling your legal obligations to pay.

Be aware that strict rules govern overtime pay and the use of "comp" time. Generally determinations as to whether employees are exempt from overtime or not are made by the HR department.

- the right to be paid within certain time frames and to be given details of pay and deductions.

- the right to make complaints about wage and hour issues without retaliation.

Benefits

- under the Employee Retirement and Income Security Act (ERISA), certain rights pertaining to pensions and other benefits. For example, employees have the right not to be terminated just so the employer can avoid providing a benefit, such as vesting in a pension plan. The subject of benefits is highly technical; you should seek expert guidance for any such questions.

Veterans' rights

Veterans enjoy special rights, including leave for certain military service and the right to return to work under certain circumstances.

Special rights of children as employees

A number of rules govern the employment of children under the age of 18. For most organizations, both federal and state laws apply, and the most restrictive law usually takes precedence.

If you are responsible for hiring young people, be sure you are aware of the restrictions; courts and juries do not look kindly upon employers who abuse the rights of children.

Be aware of work restrictions for young people in the following areas.

Hours worked

Laws restrict the number of hours in a day or the number of hours per week worked by minors. Restrictions also may limit the number of hours worked on school days, or during school sessions. Different restrictions may apply to different age groups.

Wages

Generally, children must be paid the minimum wage, although from time to time, there may be a training wage in effect, which allows pay below the minimum wage for a specified period under certain conditions.

Children generally qualify for overtime pay under the same rules as adult workers.

Types of jobs

Children are prohibited from working in hazardous occupations, and, sometimes from performing certain tasks (for example, driving). The definitions of this vary from state to state. Generally, the provisions are quite specific.

Again, restrictions are different for different age groups.

Proofs and Certificates

Some states require that minors have working papers to prove their age and their eligibility for employment. As these papers are likely to protect the employer if the child proves to be younger than you first thought, it is important to obtain these documents and have them on file as required.

Furthermore, school officials may be empowered to visit your workplace to view this documentation.

Notices

Some states require that specific notices be posted when children are employed.

Rights given by contract

Employees may have additional rights as a result of written or oral contracts or other similar agreements. (Contracts don't have to be written down to be enforceable, but it is harder to prove a contract exists if it is not written down.)

A typical written contract would be a document, signed at the beginning of employment, that details obligations of the employer and employee, the duration of the agreement, and the compensation and benefits. An offer letter that details similar information would also be such a contract.

Courts have often found an implied contract based on employee handbooks, policies, or practices. Policies detailed in an employee handbook might, for example, be viewed as guaranteeing employees the right to progressive discipline or the right to be fired only for cause. Such interpretations vary from state to state.

Rights that may be assumed

Other employee rights may not be direct legal rights, but are often implied or assumed to be rights by a court or a jury.

Right to be treated with dignity

Managers should avoid acting against employees, especially in public, to degrade or humiliate, or with explosive anger, rage, or violence.

Such behavior, especially if repeated, could contribute to a charge of "intentional infliction of emotional distress."

Right to 'good faith and fair dealing'

Some courts may recognize an obligation on the part of the employer to deal with employees at a reasonable level of good faith, regardless of whether any particular laws actually require this level of treatment.

Right to privacy

Generally, employees have few rights at work, especially if your policies so state. However, privacy rights may be assumed for areas like desks, file cabinets, lockers, and cars. It is always best to have reasonable cause to invade an employee's privacy.

It may generally be all right, for example, to look through the papers on or in an employee's desk when the employee is out and you need paperwork he or she has been working on.

Similarly, a manager may be justified in reviewing E-mail or phone messages to find out the status of a project.

However, if you've given employees passwords or suggested that messages are private, they may have a reasonable expectation of privacy. Therefore, most organizations now have a policy stating that their E-mail systems are for business use only, and that messages are not private. Such a policy may also set out the circumstances in which the employer may monitor E-mail and may require employee consent to the monitoring. By using the system, they agree that the employer has monitoring rights.

You would be wise to consult with the HR department or other experts before launching an investigation, monitoring, surveillance, and other such activity, as both federal and state laws probably apply.

Similarly, before searching locked lockers or cars, it would be wise to check with your security department or the HR office.

In conducting an investigation, you probably should ask permission to search. If your organization has a policy requiring cooperation with searches and investigations, you may discipline any employee who refuses the search.

The entire area of employee privacy rights, especially with new electronic media, is developing rapidly, and the courts are becoming increasingly interested in these rights.

Right to confidentiality of personal information

Most managers have information about employees that should not be divulged. Managers must resist the temptation to provide a juicy bit of gossip, or to make premature announcements of upcoming events.

Never reveal information from personnel records or medical records.

Never retaliate

Every manager is annoyed or angered from time to time by an employee. You may resent legally guaranteed rights —what manager wants to lose a good worker for 12 weeks of leave or likes being reported to a government agency? Retaliation may come to mind: "I'll fix that so-and-so."

Don't retaliate. It is an invitation to a lawsuit. And retaliation will never help your case—it will always seem unfair.

As with so many personnel actions, watch appearances. Don't take action that might appear to be retaliation; it can be hard to prove your true motives. For example, terminating an employee the day after he or she reports a safety violation to OSHA may be a poor idea—no matter how deserved the termination.

RESPECT EMPLOYEES' PERSONS

One of the hottest areas of legal activity in employment is the area of sexual harassment. This is a special kind of sex discrimination, in which an employee is either subjected to demands for sexual favors or made to feel uncomfortable in the workplace by sexually suggestive behaviors.

These two types of sexual harassment are called "quid pro quo" and "hostile environment."

Quid pro quo harassment

Quid pro quo (Latin for "something for something") refers to the overt behavior in which a boss demands sexual favors as a condition of getting or maintaining an employment benefit. ("Sleep with me or lose your job, your promotion, your raise.")

This form of harassment is very likely to bring a lawsuit.

Hostile environment harassment

Hostile environment harassment is harder to pinpoint, but just as dangerous from a lawsuit standpoint. If you— or your other employees—make an employee uncomfortable with unwelcome sex-based talk, jokes, touching, suggestions, etc., you have crossed the line and allowed the creation of a hostile environment—and you've encouraged an employee lawsuit.

The employee decides

Here is the most important point in sexual harassment: the judgment as to whether you've crossed that line is made by the employee. Your *intentions* don't matter—the reaction of the employee is what counts.

'But I was just joking.' You may have been joking, but that doesn't matter. If the employee was offended by your behavior, you may have created a hostile environment, whether you intended to or not.

'But they participated—they liked it!' Employees may appear to be enjoying, going along, even participating, but in court, they will often sing another tune:

"Of course I appeared to accept the behavior, of course I laughed, of course I participated. I wanted to keep my job to feed my children, so I went along."

What to do

Since you can't tell whether sexual humor or behavior is creating discomfort, your best option is to avoid it. Make sure you learn about any problems that may be going on in your department, and make sure you stop them promptly when you do discover them.

Leave sex jokes, suggestions, cartoons, magazines, teasing, and touching at the office door.

Make sure you know about your organization's grievance procedure mechanism and how to use it, and make sure to inform your employees about it. Tell them it is for them to use to make complaints about sexual harassment. Tell them you have an open door and want to hear about their problems including sexual harassment.

Employees who fail to use a clear, well-publicized, user-friendly complaint process are much less likely to be successful in a sexual harassment lawsuit.

You're responsible for keeping everyone in line

A hostile environment can be created by anyone, not just the manager. If you hear jokes, or observe inappropriate behavior, you must act. If you permit the behavior, you are condoning it.

Tell your employees as a group what you expect. If some don't respond, talk to them individually. Make it clear that you are serious. You must control this behavior in your department.

Note on office romances

Office romances have great potential to cause problems. Such relationships are rarely secret from other employees, who often perceive favoritism, whether real or imagined.

While relationships are going on, there usually isn't a problem between the partners, unless one of them has been coerced into the relationship.

However, with most relationships, eventually the breakup comes, and sometimes legal trouble along with it. An apparently willing partner now suddenly claims—and perhaps believes—that he or she was forced into the relationship. Adverse personnel actions are viewed as taking place "because we broke up." Suddenly, what seemed a normal, consenting relationship becomes quid pro quo harassment.

At a minimum, it is generally a bad idea to allow relationships between individuals with direct supervisory relationships or who have the ability to influence one another's employment status.

As for yourself, you have to decide how to run your personal life, but beware: your job is on the line.

Stop racial, religious, and ethnic comments, jokes, & slurs

As with sex-oriented comments, racial, religious, and ethnic comments and humor do not belong in the workplace. These comments can always resurface as evidence of discrimination.

Managers must refrain from saying these things, and managers must not permit or condone such behavior in subordinates.

Avoid embarrassing or humiliating employees in front of others

There are times that employees need to be told things that are embarrassing or humiliating, but there's never a need to do it in public, or to do it brutally or viciously.

CLOSE YOUR MOUTH

A big part of respecting employees—and avoiding their lawsuits—is knowing when to keep your mouth closed. And perhaps equally important is to keep your ears open. It's important to employees to know that you are paying attention.

Keep your mouth shut

Some things should never be said in the office. Period. It doesn't matter how funny or how entertaining, you just have to keep your mouth shut.

Many of the situations in which the mouth should have been kept closed have been covered above; for example,

- sex-oriented, suggestive, or lewd comments
- inappropriate teasing
- any suggestion of quid pro quo
- patronizing and discriminatory remarks
- comments about ethnic or racial stereotypes

I said it without thinking

- I'm sorry, it just slipped out.
- I said it without thinking.

These are not acceptable excuses. You're the manager; you must think.

Think ahead so you won't get caught not knowing what to say. For example, stuck with the job of laying off some longtime employees, a manager might blurt out—as a lame attempt at humor in a tough situation—

"Time for you older guys and gals to move on, I guess, eh? Make way for some younger blood. Heh Heh Heh.

With comments like these, it's heh heh all the way to the bank for the employees.

If you think through what you are going to say in these situations, you won't be tempted to try to lighten the mood with dangerous humor.

How could I know they were "wired"?

Don't ever assume that because there are no witnesses, you'll just be able to deny that you said something.

People who visit your office may be wired, that is, they may be recording your conversation without your knowledge.

It was just an E-mail note

For some reason, company electronic mail systems seem to be less formal than traditional written memos, and some managers "say" things over E-mail that they would not say in a memo, thinking that the E-mail is completely private. It's not. Furthermore, E-mail is often not erased even if it appears to have been. Experts can reconstruct old E-mail messages.

But I only said that to a customer

Customers, salespeople, and others who may be in your facility or with whom you have contact may in some cases be required to testify as to what they heard you say.

So the rule about keeping sexist and racist and age-related remarks out of the workplace goes further than your office or facility walls.

Be wary in giving references

As a manager, you are often asked for references on former employees. Before you give out any references, take the following steps:

- Familiarize yourself with your employer's policy on giving references.

- Be aware of any agreements made with employees about what the organization will say.

- In general, and especially if you are going to give derogatory information, obtain a written release from the former employee before you speak. In many organizations, the HR department would obtain this release.

In most cases, you won't get into trouble for divulging too little information, but there are cases in which you should divulge information. One, for example, is the case of a former employee discharged for violence. If this employee turns violent on a new job, you could be sued for not having revealed the information. Similar situations might include sexual offenders or child molesters, for example. If you terminate an employee for violent behavior or similarly serious action, check with your HR department for instructions about what to do when another employer calls for a reference.

OPEN YOUR EARS

Listening is a key management skill. First of all, employees want to be taken seriously. Further, you need early warning of trouble brewing. Wouldn't you like to know about the first hint of harassment so you can nip it in the bud?

They just wouldn't listen

When employees are asked why they sued, it's not unusual to hear, "Management just wouldn't listen when I tried to tell them what was going on. So I had to sue." Listening and follow-up action would have avoided such lawsuits.

Exit interviews can help

The exit interview is another opportunity to listen, and to prevent lawsuits.

First of all, employees feel freer to talk during an exit interview. They are leaving, so they have little fear of reprisal.

Second, departing employees often feel the need to "vent," to complain to someone about their situation. Would you rather have them pour out their troubles to an exit interviewer or an attorney?

A meaningful exit interview will often reveal information about problems you'd otherwise not know about until they had progressed much further. For example, you might discover that a person who appears to be resigning was actually harassed out of the company. If you find out at the exit interview, and take action, you may forestall a lawsuit.

As another example, you might discover information about the behavior of remaining employees that warrants investigation on your part.

COUNSELING IS AN IMPORTANT ROLE, BUT ...

Certainly, an important part of your role as manager is the counseling of your employees; chances are that over the years, your advice will help a great many of them. This is an area, however, in which you can get too deep in a hurry.

Be aware of your limits. You are not a trained counselor or psychiatrist. If you sense that you are over your head, it is time to back off and get help or refer the employee to your organization's Employee Assistance Program (EAP).

Do not try to play therapist.

BEYOND RESPECT—
CONTENTED EMPLOYEES DON'T SUE

Respecting your employees goes a long way toward building positive attitudes, and employee attitude has a lot to do with the motivation to sue. A contented employee is just not as likely to bring a lawsuit as a disgruntled one.

No, you don't have to coddle employees or bend to their every whim. At the same time, however, it is important to recognize that employees who feel they've been taken advantage of, cheated, pushed too hard, humiliated, done wrong, or ignored, do start to think that there must be something they can do to strike back.

Every employee who suffers doesn't file a suit. In many cases, it's because they believe that "over the years" they have been "treated right." Filing a lawsuit just doesn't occur to them.

DO YOU RESPECT YOUR EMPLOYEES?

The Parents, Spouse, Children, Little Siblings Test

Managers often ask how they can tell where "the line" is between innocent humor and teasing and illegal creation of a hostile work environment.

One expert recommends the Parents, Spouse, Children, Little Siblings Test. Before you tell a joke, tease, or engage in sexual banter, ask yourself this question: Would I be comfortable saying this with my parents, my spouse, my children, and my little brothers and sisters listening? If not, resist the temptation.

Answer these questions about your work environment:

What was the last office joke you told?

Would it pass the test?

What was the last office joke you heard?

Would it pass?

Do you engage in suggestive banter?

Would it pass?

Respect employee rights
Check if yes.

☐ Are you aware of all the various rights that your employees have?

☐ Do you know your organization's system for respectfully and meaningfully responding to employee complaints?

To whom do you report complaints, allegations, confidences?

☐ Have you placed personal restrictions on what you say?

On sexual jokes or banter?

On racial or ethnic jokes or banter?

☐ Do you put a stop to the inappropriate behavior of others in your department?

☐ Would your employees rate you as a good listener?

☐ Do you conduct exit interviews?

—Secret #4—
Share Expectations and Results

Since sharing expectations and results is probably a routine part of your performance management system, you wouldn't expect it to cause legal problems, but it often does.

There are two important factors to keep in mind as you read about sharing expectations and results.

Fairness. First, sharing expectations and results is part of being fair to employees. Juries want to know, did the employee have a chance? Did this employee know what was expected, what the standards were, what the consequences were? Regular formal and informal sharing of goals, expectations, and results, will ensure that you pass this fairness standard.

Evidence. Second, formal, written sharing of expectations and results provides necessary support for your actions should the employee involved ever file a lawsuit. It is easier to defend whatever action brought on the lawsuit if you can show that your action was based on performance or some other legitimate reason.

Formal sharing of results also demonstrates that you have been fair in letting the employee know where he or she stands.

Because of the importance of this documentation, it is crucial to be honest in your discussions of employee performance.

TELL EMPLOYEES WHAT YOU EXPECT

Tell your employees specifically what you expect of them, including the employer's rules and policies, as well as the employee's own goals and objectives.

Rules, policies, procedures

Share rules and policies with new employees, and review them regularly with all employees.

'They never told me ...'

Sometimes employees' contentions in lawsuits seem ridiculous—"They never told me they wanted me to get to work on time"—but some are more poignant—"They never told me they were displeased with my work." Juries can be swayed by the "it wasn't fair, they never told me" lament.

'Don't they know that?'

Managers tend to think, "Don't they know not to do that?" or "Surely they know that they are not meeting my expectations?" But employees often don't know, and they'll assume that everything is fine if you don't say anything.

Tell them, and you'll be sure they know. Document the fact that you told them.

Goals, standards, objectives, expectations

Your organization's performance system probably details how you set, monitor, and evaluate each employee's goals and objectives.

- Follow your system consistently. Be sure employees are familiar with their goals.

- If your system doesn't include a formal goal-setting system, write a memo documenting agreed upon goals.

- Document the fact that you have told employees of your expectations, of organization rules, of their goals or the department goals.

- Consider obtaining employee signatures, certifying that they have read and understand the contents of the document.

Personal standards and 'pet peeves'

As a manager, you're entitled to a few "pet peeves." Don't keep them a secret. Are you a stickler for punctuality, for deadlines, for phone etiquette? Tell your employees, especially new ones, what your expectations are.

Mention consequences

Be sure employees understand the consequences of their actions.

If more stringent disciplinary action will follow a repetition of misconduct, tell the employee.

If a possible promotion or bonus rides on a certain aspect of performance, tell the employee.

If you work in teams

If evaluation, compensation, bonuses, or other employee actions depend on the performance of a team as opposed to an individual, take special care in discussing the performance management system. Make sure each employee knows how the system works, and how group and individual performance is measured and compensated.

TELL EMPLOYEES—HONESTLY—HOW THEY'RE DOING

You've told your employees what you expect of them; it's just as important to make them aware—honestly aware—of how they're doing in meeting those expectations. This is accomplished through counseling, discipline, and your formal performance appraisal system.

Business reason or discrimination?

Your ability to prevent lawsuits alleging discrimination often hinges on the question of whether your actions were taken for legitimate business reasons or for discriminatory reasons. Generally, if you can show a business reason for your actions—for example, poor performance—you are more likely to win the lawsuit.

However, in many of these cases, there's a problem—you say the employee was terminated for poor performance, yet documents or actions indicate that the employee's performance was good.

This problem is a result of performance appraisal "inflation," that is, when the manager gives almost everyone top ratings, even the poor performers. Managers do this to be nice, or to get the employees bigger raises, or to avoid the unpleasantness of telling an employee that he or she is not doing well or is below average or poor in performance. However, whether this practice is well-intentioned or not, it has caused countless legal problems for employers.

What you say, or what your documents say?

Imagine yourself—perhaps on the witness stand— explaining that a termination was due to incompetence or poor production or attitude, or whatever. Then the defense attorney produces a string of performance appraisals—that you signed—indicating "excellent," or "good," or even "satisfactory." Case closed. No matter what you say now, you appear to be "lying." Your poor performance argument now appears to be a fabrication or pretense.

Actions may speak as loudly as words

Sometimes, it doesn't even take a formal document to show good performance. Just the fact that you treated the employee like other good-performing employees, that is, gave raises and bonuses, is enough to rebut your contention of poor performance.

Honest appraisals and actions

Therefore, difficult as it may be, you must be honest in your performance appraisals. Similarly, you must take appropriate disciplinary action when employees break the rules.

APPRAISAL TIPS

If you are not sure how to approach an appraisal, here is a system that many managers have found to be effective.

This assumes that you have established goals and have measured the employee's degree of success in meeting them.

Written Assessment by Manager and Employee

First, both the manager and the employee write an assessment of the employee's progress against the previously-established goals.

These reports are exchanged several days before the scheduled performance appraisal meeting. Exchanging appraisals before the meeting allows for any emotional reaction to subside, and for managers and employees to reflect on their initial assessment.

Positive Agreement Discussion

At the meeting, discuss your performance assessments using the order suggested below, starting with positive agreement. This helps set up an atmosphere of sharing that makes the discussion of poor performance a little easier to initiate.

Positive Agreement

First discuss areas of performance or specific goals for which you and the employee agree on the level of performance and agree that the performance was good.

Negative Agreement

Next, discuss areas of performance or specific goals for which you and the employee agree on the level of performance and agree that the performance was not good.

Disagreement

Finally, discuss areas in which you disagree about performance. Usually, the situation is that the employee believes that he or she did a good job, but you believe otherwise.

During this discussion, focus on observed behaviors, figures, facts, and not on personalities. (days late, dollars short rather than you're lazy or you don't care).

Agreement

Try to reach agreement on the performance in these areas in which you disagreed on first pass.

Future Goals

Next, work on goals for the future. Answer any questions about the employee's future, organization prospects, or whatever the employee wants to know about.

Many approaches to performance appraisal

Many managers have found that the combination of manager and employee exchanging appraisals ahead of time, and then following the positive agreement order of discussion during the appraisal meeting is productive.

However, there are many other effective approaches to performance management. Chances are, your organization has a program in place. Work with it, of course, but work on it also, so that you can deliver honest appraisals while encouraging better performance.

ARE YOUR APPRAISALS FAIR AND HONEST?

Fair

Do your employees know what is expected of them at work?

- ☐ Rules
- ☐ Policies
- ☐ Procedures
- ☐ Goals
- ☐ Standards
- ☐ Other expectations

Can you demonstrate that they know?

Are expectations measurable?

Do employees know the consequences of failing to meet goals?

Have you ever heard, "You never told me"?

Have you ever been surprised that employees didn't know something that you thought was obvious?

Honest

Are you committed to telling employees honestly how they are doing?

Have you ever been guilty of appraisal inflation?

—Secret #5—
Back Off, Ask for Help

Every manager faces situations that seem to demand immediate action, and the temptation is to "be a manager" and take strong action, even when you're not quite sure what the action should be. In these cases, it is often best to take *no* action, to back off, to cool down, and to get help.

Acting too quickly, without thinking a situation through, or without seeking advice, can be dangerous. Furthermore, it's often in the organization's best interest for you to seek advice and make a joint decision, even if you know your choice of action is the right action to take.

IMMEDIATE REACTION RARELY NECESSARY

Fortunately, your final, detailed decision on a tough situation is *not* required immediately. You always have time to back off, reflect, and seek advice.

Action of *some* kind may be required—as when someone is physically threatened, or when there is a significant safety concern. Frequently, an *acknowledgment* of the situation may be required, as in the case of an employee's public insubordination. However, decisions such as what type of punishment to administer or whether termination is required need not—and in fact should not—be reached at the instant when a situation presents itself.

BACK OFF, COOL OFF

When you feel pressure to make a decision you know you're not ready to make, or you're not sure how to make, back off and cool off. Take the time to make the right decision.

Act after calm consideration

Managers are often upset or angry at the moment when tough employment situations present themselves.

Perhaps employees have been insubordinate, or broken important rules, or failed to produce up to capacity, or failed to get out an order you promised to a customer. Maybe they've just embarrassed you in front of management or other employees.

Such situations may make you angry, and the anger may be justified, but angry is not the frame of mind to be in when making critical employment decisions.

Anger leads to ill-considered decisions, irresponsible public humiliation of an employee, or other unacceptable behavior, and, ultimately, to a lawsuit.

No matter how angry you are, you *must* stay in control of yourself and the situation. If your outburst ultimately costs the organization $100,000 in legal fees, how far do you think your excuse, "Well, gosh, I was angry," will get you?

Why a delay is important

Delaying final action is important for reasons beyond emotion and anger.

- **Don't know.** First of all, managers often don't know what the appropriate action is in a given circumstance. A colleague or an HR representative, however, may be able to put a broader perspective on the situation, and ensure that it is handled consistently according to organization policy.

- **Special needs.** Furthermore, there may be a special situation that needs to be addressed. For example, if the employee in question has recently exercised a legal right and this action might be viewed as retaliation, the situation must be discussed with the HR professionals before any action is taken. For instance, has the employee in question:

    —asked for family leave?

    —become disabled or announced a pregnancy?

    —had a talk with OSHA about problems in the plant, or made any formal complaint to a government agency?

    —made allegations or complaints?

- **Other activity.** In addition, there may be other personnel actions taking place of which the immediate manager may not be aware. For example, reductions in force, reassignments, or restructurings could be planned that would affect the decision.

When to delay action

How do you know when to delay? Usually, you'll hear a "warning bell."

You'll feel uncomfortable with the situation, or you'll think, "Maybe this is one of those cases in which I should be holding off until I get some advice."

Typical situations calling for delay are listed below, but any time you're unsure, it's better to back off and call the HR department.

Delay if:

• you face unusual or confusing circumstances.

• you would have to act counter to policy.

• you feel uncomfortable.

• you believe you might be facing allegations of discrimination or retaliation.

• you are angry or emotionally charged.

• you are contemplating serious punishment or termination.

How to delay action and preserve your prerogatives

You don't have to give up your opportunity to discuss a situation, to impose discipline, or even terminate, just because you have chosen—wisely—to delay action.

Often the best course to take is to acknowledge a problem or situation, but to delay making a decision until you've backed off, cooled down, and sought advice, consulted a policy, or checked with the HR department.

For example, you might say:

"I'd like to see you in my office at three, and we'll discuss this matter."

"I'll be speaking with each of you individually before the end of the day."

"It's clear that we have a serious problem here. I want to reflect on the situation, and I will talk to you tomorrow."

A more serious step, but one which still preserves your ability to take the time to make a good decision is a suspension with pay. This removes the person from the action, and allows you to investigate, confer, do whatever is necessary before making a decision.

WHY YOU SHOULD SEEK A GROUP DECISION

Why should you consult others before acting? Even if you're sure you know what to do, it's often better to act from a consensus decision. Here's why.

- **Experts.** First of all, as mentioned, other members of your management team—for example, the HR manager—may be in a better position to judge an appropriate reaction because they are familiar with the actions the organization has taken in similar circumstances.

  In addition, they're the experts, trained to interpret organization policy and employment law.

- **Group decision.** But there is another important reason: if the action you are taking should ever be litigated, a group decision will more likely give the appearance of having been arrived at by careful consideration. The decision of a single manager may well be viewed as self-serving, emotional, or hasty and unreasoned, where the decision of a group will be more likely to appear reasoned, businesslike, and harder to mistrust.

- **Witnesses.** Furthermore, since litigation can go on for years, and since managers come and go, it's in the organization's best interest to have several managers familiar with the particulars of a situation.

Otherwise, when a case comes to trial, the only management witness may be long gone.

TIPS FOR THE NEW SUPERVISOR OR MANAGER

New managers are often overwhelmed by the many new duties of a managerial job. This is an especially important time to bear in mind that you may back off and get help when presented with a problem. Don't act when you don't know what to do, and don't answer questions when you don't know the answer.

If you've just been appointed to managerial duties, make sure you get some training. If you make a major mistake, you'll pay the price.

Learn your organization's policies and practices. Meet with the HR manager to go over your responsibilities, and any special areas of concern that may be particular to your department, your organization, or any of your employees.

You probably can't cover everything at once, but before you hire, check on hiring, and before you appraise, check on appraisals, and so on.

SHOULD YOU BACK OFF?

☐ Have you experienced situations in which you made a hasty decision you later regretted?

What could you have done differently?

☐ Do you now recognize that you may always back off and cool off and seek advice before you act?

☐ Write here the names and numbers of people to call for:

• Administrative questions
and requests _____

• Violence and security issues _____

• Labor and union questions _____

• Drug and alcohol use _____

• Discipline and termination _____

• Complaints and allegations _____

☐ Do you recognize the importance of making a group decision before taking serious personnel actions?

—Secret #6—
Take Action When Necessary

The last section talked about backing off and taking no action. But sometimes failing to act—when action is called for—can create legal problems as devastating as taking the wrong action or taking no action.

Some managers worry so much about doing the wrong thing that they do nothing. Some don't know that they should be doing something. And others either don't bother or find the required act uncomfortable, and never get around to it.

DO YOUR DUTY

Management responsibilities such as discipline, negative performance appraisals, termination, reference checks and harassment investigations are not the fun part of the job, but when they are necessary, they *must* be performed.

Failures to act, such as those listed below, have been the cause of many lawsuits.

CONDUCT THOROUGH REFERENCE CHECKS

This one of the most common places in which managers fail to act, and, as mentioned above, one of the most dangerous. A lawsuit alleging "negligent hiring" is what might happen when you fail to check references. It typically applies to violent behavior. For example, if someone in your office commits an act of violence, the question is, did you do what a reasonable person should have done to find out about this person before you hired him or her? If you should have known (by routine reference and background checks) that a person had a history of violence, and you didn't do the check, you could be liable.

REACT TO MOUNTING SIGNS OF VIOLENCE, MENTAL INSTABILITY, OR SUBSTANCE ABUSE

Failure to act in this situation might result in charges of "negligent retention" or "negligent supervision." If you ignore signs that a reasonable person should have seen and reacted to, you may be in trouble.

TAKE ALLEGATIONS SERIOUSLY

Failure to respond quickly and meaningfully to allegations may result in two problems: it may cause resentment in the complainer and it may tell a judge and jury that you didn't care.

The effectiveness of quick response has been demonstrated most dramatically in sexual harassment situations, but it applies generally to all allegations of misconduct and illegal acts.

Respond quickly and appropriately

In a number of cases, when employers responded immediately and took corrective action, where appropriate, to allegations of harassment, they won lawsuits that might otherwise have been lost.

Important points in their successes:

(1) Management hadn't known of the harassment before the employee brought it to their attention, and

(2) The managers' response was meaningful—they investigated thoroughly and they took appropriate action based on policy and training.

From the employee's standpoint, lack of a response causes great resentment; in many lawsuits, the non-response of management pushed the employee to sue.

For most managers, the best action to take in the event of an allegation of harassment or misconduct is to contact the HR department. Investigations in these circumstances are delicate and should be done only by professional HR staff members designated with this responsibility, or under their guidance.

Take appropriate action upon conclusion of the investigation

Many times an investigation is conducted promptly, but the organization fails to take appropriate corrective action.

Perhaps there is a hope that "everyone will forget the whole thing," or that "since we've done an investigation, everyone will know we're serious, it'll never happen again."

Maybe it was a "he said/she said" situation in which no one knew what to do next so nothing was done.

Maybe management was embarrassed.

As noted above, this lack of response will not sit well with the employee who complained, and it won't sit well with the court. That employee, who wasn't looking for a lawsuit, who just wanted to stop offensive behavior, is transformed into an angry "they-ignored-my-complaint-they-think-I'm-nothing-I'm-going-to-sue" litigant.

DEAL FIRMLY AND CONSISTENTLY WITH MISCONDUCT

Take great care in dealing with serious discipline problems such as theft or other misconduct which may invoke tough penalties or termination.

Discipline favored employees as you have disciplined others

Every manager has favorites, often those with whom the manager is friends, or those who perform exceptionally well. If you fail to discipline them for offenses for which you have disciplined others, you'll lose consistency and fairness.

When the employees who were disciplined accuse you in court of disciplining them because they were old, or female, or whatever, what will you say?

Terminate when termination is warranted

Termination is a difficult responsibility for most managers. It's easy to put it off, hoping that things will get better or the person will "take a hint" and leave the organization. But if you don't act, you are tolerating the behavior, and eventually condoning and accepting it. Then, when you finally do terminate, it becomes harder to rebut a claim of discrimination. "You allowed him to do it for over a year; how can it suddenly now be a terminable offense?"

Note: See detailed discussion of steps to take before terminating above in "Secret #2—Be Fair to All Employees."

Document problems

When there's no record of misbehavior or unsatisfactory performance, and no record of having talked to the employee about it, it's hard to suggest that misbehavior was a problem. If there *is* a record of "satisfactory" performance ratings, there's little you can do to convince anyone that there was a performance problem. In the face of a lawsuit alleging discrimination, you're going to look silly with no notes, no dates, no proof. Here is what the jury hearing such a case might be thinking:

"You took the time and trouble to make a written record of the satisfactory behavior every six months, and you're trying to tell us that some unsatisfactory behavior, for which you didn't take the time to make a record, was important enough to warrant termination?"

Adhere to union contract provisions

In a unionized organization, a variety of clauses in the union contract may govern or impact the ways in which you may discipline or otherwise treat your employees. For example, employees may have the right to be accompanied by a union representative during a disciplinary meeting.

In a unionized situation, consult with HR before taking serious actions affecting employees.

DO YOU TAKE NECESSARY ACTION?

Have you ever delayed action on a personnel issue because you

☐ Didn't know what to do?

☐ Because you hoped the problem would go away?

☐ Because the thought of taking the action made you uncomfortable?

Have you hired, and later regretted not doing more thorough reference checks?

I know that I must

☐ Respond quickly and meaningfully to allegations of harassment or discrimination.

☐ Discipline and or terminate when warranted.

☐ Consistently document problems.

☐ Conduct thorough reference checks before hiring.

☐ Take appropriate action upon conclusion of the investigation.

☐ React to mounting signs of violence, mental instability, or substance abuse.

—Secret #7—
Keep Careful Records

In many lawsuits, the biggest challenge is trying to prove you took a certain action, when you have poor or nonexistent documentation. Documentation is recorded information, including letters, notes, notices, and memoranda.

For example, you'll often want to prove that an employee:

- was given a warning.
- committed certain acts at certain times.
- knew of a certain rule or expectation.
- received particular training.
- was placed on some type of probationary status.

If you have documented your actions and observations, you can prove what took place.

WHAT DOES A DOCUMENT PROVE?

Does a document actually prove anything? Will my notes be accepted in court?

If you can show that your documentation is consistent and reliable, your written word, recorded at the time of an action, is likely to be accepted as true.

Furthermore, it's far better than no documentation at all. If you don't have any record of having done something, the more you insist you did it, the more it may appear that you're making it up.

HOW TO KEEP YOUR RECORDS

If you observe infractions, if you impose discipline, if you notify employees of needed changes in behavior, if you set goals, if you appraise or counsel, document your actions. Make detailed, accurate memos of your actions and observations, and make the notes at the time of the action or soon thereafter.

Detailed

Record in some detail what took place. For example, a note such as "discussed Joe's performance with him" is much weaker and more vague than a listing of areas of weakness or specific recommendations for improvement. Be sure to do the following:

- Note dates, times, places, witnesses, etc.
- Record what the employee is expected to do in response.
- Record what you will do if the employee fails to respond or improve.

Accurate

Be sure what you write is accurate. If any part of your document is proven wrong, the validity of the entire document is called into question.

Current

Write your memo right away, and be sure to date it. So-called "contemporaneous" records carry much more weight than those created after the fact, which may appear more like fabrication than documentation.

ACTIONS TO DOCUMENT

Typical documentation would include the following:

• Receipt and understanding of policy and orientation documents.

• Attendance rosters for training sessions.

• Infractions of work rules.

• Complaints about the employee by others, such as sex harassment complaints, as well as records reflecting your response, results of an investigation, and so on.

• Steps taken for discipline problems.

• Performance appraisals and significant discussions.

Must I document *everything*?

No, you'd go nuts trying to document every little thing you ever said to any employee. You have to be the judge of the significance of your interactions with your employees. The important thing is to find a reasonable level to document at and then to be consistent in accomplishing it for all employees.

NEVER FALSIFY A DOCUMENT

Never falsify, backdate, or alter any document. If the temptation presents itself, resist it. First of all, it is not likely that you can get away with it; second, the penalties will be severe; and third, you're likely to lose your case.

BUILDING A 'PAPER CASE'

When you want to fire an employee, but the record shows satisfactory performance, or contains no hint of problems, someone may suggest to you that you start "building a case" against the problem employee by documenting everything the employee does wrong. This action surely will increase your evidence of poor performance and will help you to support termination.

Unfortunately, however, there's a trap here. If you focus on documenting only one employee's shortcomings, that could end up helping to prove a claim of discrimination. It will certainly appear that the employee was singled out for this special treatment, and that you were "out to get" the employee.

It's better to follow the rule of consistency—when infractions occur, write them up for every employee who commits them, not just one.

IS YOUR DOCUMENTATION ADEQUATE?

Have you ever needed to prove an event took place and discovered that you had no paperwork to back you up?

Have you had an employee say, "Gee I didn't know I was supposed to do that," when you know otherwise, but can't prove it?

Commit yourself to documenting significant employee interactions. Check the following aspects of your personnel record-keeping operation. Do you document:

- ❏ Participation in orientation sessions and performance management meetings covering expectations?

- ❏ Distribution and discussion of required notifications to employees, including the employee handbook and any revisions to it?

- ❏ Training on such topics as safety, violence, and sexual harassment?

- ❏ Performance appraisals? Are they honest? Do you share them with the employee? In the event of a wrongful discharge claim by an employee terminated for poor performance, would your appraisals support the termination?

- ❏ Misconduct you witness? Do you communicate this to the employee involved?

- ❏ Any disciplinary action you take?

—IV—
Summary

Seven secrets. They're not hard—and they do make a difference. Having read the book, you know the basic rules. Follow them in your dealings with your employees. And from now on, when you approach a difficult task, like hiring or firing, look it up in the next section of the book to refresh your memory.

<u>YOU</u> CAN AVOID EMPLOYEE LAWSUITS

#1—Hire People Who Won't Sue

#2—Be Fair to <u>All</u> Employees

#3—Treat Employees with Respect

#4—Share Expectations and Results

#5—Take Action When Necessary

#6—Back Off, Ask for Help

#7—Keep Careful Records

—V—

Quick Reference—
Employment Actions

Before you interview, appraise, discipline, or fire, look up the topic here, and remind yourself of the do's and don'ts.

QUICK TABLE OF CONTENTS

HIRING NEW EMPLOYEES

Remember, this is your best opportunity to avoid employee lawsuits.

Know the rules

Your organization probably has policies governing many aspects of the hiring process, including such things as applicant flow, immigration law compliance, and so on. Before you set out to hire a new employee:

- ☐ Check with the HR department to be sure that you know what the policies and procedures are.

- ☐ Find out what your specific obligations are.

Setting requirements

- ☐ Know what you're looking for; otherwise, it is hard to justify any of your decisions.

- ☐ Set job-oriented, specific criteria drawn from the requirements of the job.

- ☐ Avoid mention of any prohibited criterion (for example, age, sex, or race).

- ☐ If you have any standards which require residence, language facility, or certain physical characteristics, check with HR department before proceeding.

Soliciting applicants

- ☐ Determine the breadth of your search (nationwide, regional, or local).

- ☐ Cast a wide net. Be sure that in combination, the techniques you use expose the opening to a wide, full range of potential applicants.

- ☐ Avoid mention of any prohibited characteristic (for example, age, sex, or race).

- ❏ Avoid use of terms such as waitress or busboy that seem to call for only one sex.

- ❏ Avoid a narrow approach, such as just asking a group of colleagues for suggestions, that could exclude large groups of possible candidates.

- ❏ Follow your organization's policy governing internal and external search.

Evaluating resumés

In evaluating resumés and selecting which applicants to interview:

- ❏ Stay job-focused—what are the requirements of the job, how well can these candidates fulfill them?

- ❏ Think, could I justify on the basis of the job requirements the choices I have made?

Interviewing

- ❏ Prepare questions for all candidates that will help you to explore their

    —experiences

    —backgrounds

    —skills

    —approaches to your problems.

- ❏ Ask these questions consistently of all candidates.

- ❏ Prepare special questions for each individual candidate based on what you find in each resumé and from other sources.

- ❏ Record your notes during or immediately after the interview.

Interview questions

As you prepare questions, either before or during the interview, remember these areas in which restrictions or prohibitions apply. Detailed explanations for this material are found above in the section of the book entitled, "Be Fair to All Employees."

Restricted or prohibited—personal characteristics
- ☐ Age
- ☐ Sex
- ☐ Race or color
- ☐ Photos
- ☐ Height and weight
- ☐ Disabilities
- ☐ Sickness and attendance
- ☐ Availability

Restricted or prohibited—background
- ☐ Birthplace and citizenship
- ☐ Residence
- ☐ Marital status
- ☐ Name/name change
- ☐ Personal finances
- ☐ Relatives
- ☐ Religion

Restricted or prohibited—education and experience
- ☐ Education
- ☐ Language
- ☐ Military service

- ❑ Organizations, Clubs, Associations
- ❑ Arrest records

Testing

- ❑ Be sure tests you give are approved by your HR department. (Varying and technical state requirements govern the legality of testing.)
- ❑ Give the test to all candidates.
- ❑ Evaluate the results of test consistently for all candidates.

Selecting

- ❑ Stick to evaluating the criteria you've established for the position.

Reference checking

- ❑ Call references with business connections.
- ❑ Call former supervisors.
- ❑ Consider
    - —credit
    - —police
    - —other background checks.

Take special care with your records and background checks if you have:

- ❑ positions in which individual employees visit clients in their homes.
- ❑ safety-sensitive positions such as bus drivers.
- ❑ positions in which adults work with children.

❑ When questioning references, avoid any questions that would be considered improper in the interview (such as those concerning race, marital status, personal finances, etc.).

Offers of employment/offer letters

❑ Follow the recommendations of your HR department or let them handle the offer.

❑ Avoid making promises you can't deliver.

❑ If unusual promises or representations have been made, spell them out so there will be no misunderstanding later.

❑ Avoid creating a contract if you don't want to.

Child Labor

Strict rules govern the hiring of children and young people in most states. If you employ or intend to employ young people, check your state law carefully in these areas.

Note that the rules generally change with different age brackets.

Check to see if you are covered by any of these types of restrictions:

❑ Time of day that work is permitted.

❑ Number of hours per day.

❑ Number of hours per week.

❑ School day restrictions.

❑ Type of work permitted.

❑ Any other restriction.

❑ Certificates required to be posted.

❑ Posters required to be posted.

ORIENTING NEW EMPLOYEES

The orientation period is important for insuring that certain information is imparted and that there are no misconceptions.

Note: Many of these actions may be taken care of by the HR department in your organization.

- ☐ Review the agreement you have with the employee, including salary, benefits, pay periods, and so on.

- ☐ Ask, have any other representations or promises been made to you concerning your employment here? If there are additional promises, and if they may violate policy or be hard to keep, clarify the situation right away.

- ☐ Go over the organization's rules and regulations.

- ☐ Clarify your expectations.

- ☐ Avoid promises that are going to be hard to keep.

- ☐ Avoid off-the-cuff statements such as "Don't mess up and you'll be here until you retire," or "We take care of our own, we never terminate unless there is just cause."

- ☐ Insure that new employees read and sign all necessary documents. Many organizations provide a checklist for this function.

Documents which might require signature:

- ☐ Sheet indicating that the employee has received and read the employee handbook.

- ☐ Trade secret agreements.

- ☐ Inventions agreement.

- ☐ Non-compete agreement.

- ☐ Any other type of agreement you use.

TRAINING AND DEVELOPMENT

In this arena, the most important consideration is fairness. When selecting employees for:

- special assignments,
- promotions,
- projects,
- task forces, or
- teams,
  - ☐ Focus on job-related criteria.
  - ☐ Be sure that decisions are fair.

Be sure all eligible employees know:

- ☐ what is required for consideration and for selection,
- ☐ how to apply or be considered, and
- ☐ how to prepare themselves for consideration.

Check your decisions over the past year or two to be sure that you don't give the appearance of discriminating, even though each individual decision may be supportable in your mind.

SETTING GOALS AND APPRAISING EMPLOYEES

Managers who don't pay enough attention to the goal-setting and appraisal process often create fertile ground for a successful lawsuit. Here is what to do:

Goal-setting

☐ Set clear, agreed-upon goals.

☐ Insure that the employee knows and understands what the goals are and accepts the goals.

☐ Be sure that the employee knows, at least in a general way, the consequences of failing to meet the goals.

Appraisal

☐ Be honest in evaluating employees' performance.

☐ Discuss performance with employees regularly, and be sure that they know how they are doing.

☐ Be aware of the trap of "being nice" and giving ratings higher than deserved.

☐ Be sure that your performance discussions are clearly documented.

Check yourself on fairness by looking over your appraisals for the past year.

☐ Rank your employees—to the extent that you can compare them—on their performance.

☐ Go over your appraisal ratings to see if they reflect the ranking.

☐ Check to ensure that you have been consistent in your rankings.

☐ If compensation is dependent upon ratings, check to ensure that your compensation decisions have been consistent with rankings.

COMPENSATING EMPLOYEES

Compensation is primarily an issue of fairness. The regulations governing exemption and overtime do add a legal issue to compensation.

Lay out a roster of your employees by grade and position, including salary history. Note race, age, sex for each employee. Use this listing to insure that you are consistent and fair in your compensation decisions. Check for cases in which:

- [ ] Any group of employees (e.g., all female, all young, or all black) seems to be paid more or less than the others.

- [ ] Raises are extra high or extra low for any group. These are red flags that might indicate discrimination.

- [ ] There might be an appearance of discrimination, even though there was no discriminatory intent.

- [ ] You have off-the-books arrangements with employees concerning overtime or compensatory time. (These could backfire on you. You probably owe the employee the money, and if the arrangement has been going on for years with several employees, the amount could be staggering.)

- [ ] Any of your employees do anything for your benefit for which you do not pay them (for example, work extra hours, or do errands on their way home). Check with the HR department to be sure you are fulfilling your legal obligations to pay.

EMPLOYEES' REQUESTS AND COMPLAINTS

Personnel administration is primarily a matter of taking employee concerns seriously, maintaining confidentiality, and following policy.

Respect employee concerns

☐ When an employee makes a request for leave, jury duty, or other action, take it seriously. Evaluate it, seek help if you need to from HR specialists, and give the employee a reply within a reasonable period.

Respect employee complaints

☐ Take employee complaints seriously. If you fail to do this, you make the situation worse. Also, remember that in many instances, the employee's right to complain is protected, so do not retaliate in any way.

☐ Respond quickly to allegations of misconduct or harassment and take appropriate action. If you have been trained in what to do, go ahead. Otherwise, immediately report to the HR department and seek their advice. You or they will probably have to conduct an investigation.

☐ See the section in the main text on "Respect employee rights" for more detailed information.

Maintain confidentiality

☐ Maintain the confidentiality of all records and other information you have.

Follow policy

☐ When confronted with employee requests or complaints, follow your organization policy. "Shooting from the hip" and making up policy as you go along is courting disaster.

DISCIPLINING EMPLOYEES

- ☐ Know the rules. Follow your organization's discipline system.

- ☐ Avoid sudden decisions made in anger.

- ☐ Do not terminate or threaten termination without seeking advice.

- ☐ Conduct discipline discussions in private or with another member of management present.

- ☐ Try to keep observations job-oriented.

- ☐ Allow the employee an opportunity to explain.

- ☐ Seek help when you aren't sure what to do or when a serious situation arises.

- ☐ Be consistent. Impose the same punishment for similarly-situated employees for the same offense.

- ☐ Be reasonable. Impose discipline that a reasonable person would agree was appropriate.

- ☐ Be equal. Ensure that your actions are consistent and reasonable across the various protected classes of employees.

- ☐ Be careful. If the person to be disciplined is female, older, from a certain race or national origin, religion, disabled, or a veteran, is there any evidence that this discipline could have been influenced by that fact? Or might it appear to have been influenced by that fact? Get advice.

TERMINATING EMPLOYEES

Termination is a prime danger spot for employee lawsuits. If your answer to any question below calls the termination into question, seek assistance from the HR department.

Layoffs

In general, if you intend to lay off employees, check with the HR department for guidance. Federal and state laws, as well as seniority and other practices may need to be observed.

Look at the group of employees to be laid off in relation to the employees who will be left. Is there anything to suggest bias on the basis of:

- ☐ Race,
- ☐ Sex,
- ☐ Religion,
- ☐ Age, or
- ☐ Disability?

Terminations for cause

Ask yourself the following questions.

- ☐ Are you about to act in anger or under the influence of strong emotions?
- ☐ Is this the appropriate punishment for the offense? Would a jury consider it reasonable?
- ☐ Is this a consistent punishment? That is, has the same punishment been given to all others who committed the same offense?

- [ ] Does the person you are about to fire belong to a protected class? That is, is the person female, older, from a certain race, national origin, or religion, disabled, or a veteran? If so, is there any evidence that this termination could have been influenced by that fact? Or might it appear to have been influenced by that fact?
- [ ] Have you made any promises to this person with which this action might conflict?
- [ ] Is this action related to off-duty conduct?
- [ ] Is there any chance this could have been concerted activity? That is, done on behalf of other employees, or in concert with them? (This could be protected union activity.)
- [ ] Is this a timely action, or have weeks gone by since the infraction?
- [ ] Is any retaliation claim possible?
- [ ] Is the employee about to qualify for a benefit?
- [ ] Did the person recently complain to a government agency, etc.?
- [ ] Did the person have notice of the termination?
- [ ] Is there any suggestion that you're trying to get rid of the person for personal reasons?
- [ ] Have you conducted an investigation? Are you sure that you have the facts right?
- [ ] Is the employee who is to be terminated a long-term employee?
- [ ] Has the employee had a chance to explain?
- [ ] If you gave warning, did the employee have a chance to improve?

❑ Do performance appraisals support your decision?

❑ Is this action consistent with actions you have taken with others who have the same performance profile?

❑ Do you have records, witnesses?

❑ Is your termination based on the results of a lie detector test, surveillance, or other action which may not be legal?

❑ If there is the potential of trouble, do you need a witness present during the termination?

—Appendix A—
What You Should Know About State Law

The concepts in this book—the seven secrets—are based both on the requirements of federal law and, in a general way, on the requirements of state law.

However, state laws covering various aspects of the employment relationship differ from state to state.

Furthermore, state courts often differ in their application of basic areas of law which apply to employment, such as laws dealing with contracts.

The basic principles presented in this book, for example, being fair and treating employees with respect, apply in all states. However, it is up to you to determine the requirements of the particular laws in your state.

For example, the eligibility rules of some states' family leave laws are different from those of the federal law. Some states' laws provide different benefits and durations. As another example, some state courts have been more willing than others to acknowledge as enforceable contracts the statements made in employee handbooks. Some states include sexual orientation as a protected category; others do not.

What should you do to be sure you know how the rules apply in your state?

❑ Review the state law checklist on the following page.

❑ Meet with your HR department to learn about state law requirements.

❑ Ask for help before making final decisions.

For more detailed guidance, consider BLR's *Quick Guide to Employment Law* (Federal and 50 states and Washington, D.C., and Puerto Rico). This book provides, in comparative chart form, the federal employment laws as well as the laws of all the states, Washington, D.C., and Puerto Rico. Order from Ransom & Benjamin at 1-800-334-3352.

STATE LAW CHECKLIST

Look through this list to find areas in which your state law may differ from federal or from other states.

Discrimination

- ❑ Types of discrimination prohibited.
- ❑ Size and type of employer covered.
- ❑ Filing deadlines.
- ❑ Posting requirements.
- ❑ Provisions covering people with the HIV (human immunodeficiency virus) or with symptoms of AIDS (acquired immune deficiency syndrome).
- ❑ Provisions affecting testing of applicants.

Privacy

- ❑ Are specific actions prohibited or limited?

Employment at will

- ❑ What is your state's law on the concept of at-will employment?
- ❑ How are handbook disclaimer statements interpreted?

Compensation

- ❑ Minimum wage.
- ❑ Overtime.

Time Off/Paid and Unpaid Leave

- ❑ Leaves of absence.
- ❑ Family medical leave.

Child labor

Check to see if there are any requirements or restrictions concerning:

- ☐ Hours,
- ☐ Days,
- ☐ School days,
- ☐ Types, or
- ☐ Certificates.

HR administration

- ☐ Record-keeping requirements.
- ☐ Notices and posting requirements.

Safety and health

- ☐ Safety programs.
- ☐ Safety posters.

Workers' Compensation

Check specific aspects of your state law with regard to:

- ☐ Eligibility.
- ☐ Procedures.
- ☐ Retaliation provisions.

—Appendix B—
Trainer's Guide

There are a variety of ways in which this book can be incorporated into managerial training programs.

YOUR PREPARATION

Whatever method of presentation you use, you will have to do some preparation yourself.

I. Get to know the book and its concepts.

First of all, to use this book as a training tool, you must familiarize yourself with the book and its seven secrets— that is, the seven basic concepts the book presents.

In addition, familiarize yourself with the exercises at the end of each section.

2. Relate to your organization.

To provide the most effective training, connect the concepts in the book with the operations of your organization.

- Review lawsuits and charges brought against your organization. Use these to build your presentation.

(You probably do not want to discuss actual cases, or use real names.)

- Review your organization policies and determine which need to be presented.

- Review your organization's employee handbook to see what policies need to be mentioned or referred to.

- Think through your state laws and how to fit that information into the training.

- If your industry has special rules, plan how to integrate them into the training.

SELECT A METHOD OF PRESENTATION

How will you present the material? One quick session? Several longer sessions? Eight sessions spread out over eight months?

There are many approaches to presenting training; you must decide which one will work best for your organization. The suggestions which follow will assist you.

NO FORMAL TRAINING SESSION

The simplest approach is to hand out the book, ask managers to read it, and then hold a discussion period during a regularly scheduled managers' meeting. During the discussion, managers may comment on the book and ask follow-up questions

If you choose this method, be sure to schedule a time at a future meeting for managers to comment on the book or ask questions.

SINGLE SESSION

The next level of training would be to schedule a single session of one to two hours on the issues raised in the book. The meeting would include a presentation and discussion of the concepts; completion of one or two of the exercises, and a few minutes for specific examples and materials from your organization.

There are two approaches to this session: having the participants read the book before attending the training, or having them read after the session. Either can work.

Read the book beforehand

In this case you will review the concepts, answer questions, discuss applications, and provide specific information about your organization's policies and practices, and your experiences with past lawsuits.

Read the book afterwards

With this approach, you will present the concepts at one meeting, and have your managers read the book on their own.

This will be most effective if you schedule a follow-up session at which managers share their reactions to the book and ask questions.

SUGGESTED OUTLINE—SINGLE SESSION

- Introduce the book with the "million dollar mouth" examples from the first section of the book.

- Explain why it is in your managers' best interest to learn to how to avoid lawsuits.

- Discuss juries and how they think.

- Discuss and clarify the concept that it is each individual manager's responsibility to avoid lawsuits.
- Complete the exercise at the end of the first section of the book. ("How much will your lawsuit cost?")
- Gain your managers' commitment to focus on this training and put it to use in their management.
- Go over the "secrets" one by one, answering questions as you go.
- Cover any special aspects involving your organization's business, special policies, or special problems..
- Summarize with the admonition, "Above all, be fair."

SUGGESTED OUTLINE—SEVERAL SESSIONS

The most effective training is accomplished over a period of time. For example, spend the first fifteen minutes of each monthly management meeting on this training, following a schedule similar to the one presented below.

Meeting I—Why this is important

- Introduce the book with the "million dollar mouth" examples. What are some of the things managers do to provoke employee lawsuits?
- Explain why it is in your managers' best interest to learn to avoid lawsuits.
- Discuss juries and how they think.
- Discuss and clarify the concept that it is each individual manager's responsibility to avoid lawsuits.
- Complete the exercise at the end of the first section of the book. ("How much will your lawsuit cost?")

- Gain your managers' commitment to focus on this training and put it to use in their management.

Meetings 2-8—Cover the secrets one-by-one

Since some of the secrets are much more detailed than others, you probably won't actually stick to doing one each session. Secrets #2 and #3 will probably be worth two sessions each.

For each secret, complete the exercise that follows, or substitute some exercise more related to your operations or particular situation.

Meeting 9—Present materials specific to your organization and summarize training

Materials specific to your organization include:

- Lawsuits you have had or are concerned about.

- Your state law and its particular requirements.

- Industry rules or practices.

- Policies governing employee actions.

- Your recruiting process.

- Systems for training, development, and appraisal.

- Procedures for discipline and termination.

Summarize the training for participants with these three admonitions:

- Think of the jury.

- Be fair.

- Ask for help before you take any action you might regret.

Allow some time to answer participants' questions.

CONCLUSION

Whichever training program you select, you will be a successful trainer if you follow the preparation suggestions in the beginning of this appendix on training.

Be sure that you follow the basics of good training as well: conduct the training in a comfortable setting, free from interruptions. Be sure that all required equipment and materials are in place. Arrange for refreshments if appropriate.

Managers who follow the principles in this book will avoid employee lawsuits. It is the trainer's job to be sure the managers study the principles, understand them, and know the situations in which they apply.

Best wishes!

Notes